For the Love of ACT Reading

Tehya Baxter
Kyla Haggerty
Dan Hamilton
Emily Lubejko

ISBN-13: 978-0-9968322-7-4

Published by Private Prep
Printed by kindle direct publishing, An Amazon.com Company
Edited by Michele O'Brien & Andrew Dahl
Version 2022-2023

Contents

Chapter 1

Getting Started

Look out for handwritten annotations as you read! Marking the text is a great way to stay focused on key information.

Key Topics
- Welcome! - The Basics of ACT Reading - ACT Reading Diagnostic Exam - Your Study Timeline

1.1 Welcome to *For the Love of ACT Reading*!

Let's get right to it. You've heard about the ACT Reading section. *Everyone runs out of time! More than one answer could be correct! My friend misread a bunch of the questions!* It's true: ACT Reading can be tricky, but you will learn strategies to handle the test with confidence.

There are three main factors that can make the ACT Reading section a challenge for students:

- You don't have much time.
- Some *questions* are deceptively tricky.
- Some *answer choices* are deceptively tricky.

BUT, here is the good news about the ACT Reading section:

- The questions are quite predictable and fit into clearly defined categories.
- The ACT is less concerned with the type of analysis you might be used to doing in your English class and far more concerned with specific details and summary. That makes your job a little easier!
- The test is multiple choice, so there can only be one correct answer.
- Like every section on the ACT, there is no guessing penalty. This means that even if you're making a complete guess, you still have a chance of picking up the point! Bubble in an answer for every single question. If you leave a question blank, it will automatically be scored as incorrect.

This book is your key to feeling in control of the ACT Reading section. It will help you become a master of...

- **Reading:** what to read, how to read it, and what to look out for as you do
- **Timing:** how to manage the fast pace of the section
- **Questions:** how to break down complex questions
- **Answer Choices:** how to avoid common traps and choose correct answers with process of elimination, close reading, and guessing strategies

As you read, you'll learn to recognize the patterns of the ACT Reading section. With practice, the section will feel like an old friend. When it comes time to sit for the real test, there won't be any surprises. Though you won't know if your Natural Science passage will be about snowflakes or snowshoe hares, you'll be equipped with tools that will help you manage whatever the section throws your way! Again, this is a Very. Predictable. Section. By getting to know it, you can improve your score.

1.2 The Basics of ACT Reading

The directions at the beginning of the ACT Reading section never change. Read them once now; then, you can skip them from here on out!

10 per passage!

READING TEST

35 Minutes — 40 Questions

DIRECTIONS: There are four passages in this test. Each passage is followed by several questions. Choose the best answer to each question and fill in the corresponding oval on your answer document. You may refer to the passages as often as necessary.

What kinds of passages are on the ACT Reading section?
Here they are, in the order you'll see them on each test:

Passage Genre in Order of Appearance	What to Expect...	Example Topic
Literary Narrative	An excerpt from a fictional story (though often without a traditional beginning, middle, and end)	How a memorable afternoon at summer camp shaped a young girl's understanding of herself
Social Science	A nonfiction passage about society (history, government, economics)	Questioning the relevance of using paper in contemporary society
Humanities	A nonfiction passage about the arts (music, dance, literature, photography) or an autobiography or memoir	A memoir detailing the writing process of an author's debut novel
Natural Science	A nonfiction passage about science (specific studies, animals, or phenomena)	An explanation of a new theory about the birth of stars

In every ACT Reading section, you can also expect to see one **paired passage**. This simply means that one of the passages will actually consist of two shorter, related passages (instead of a single, longer passage). The 10 questions will be divided into questions about Passage A, questions about Passage B, and then Comparative Questions that refer to both passages.

Bad news? The paired passage can show up in any of the four genres, so you can't predict its location.

Good news? It only appears once per section!

Better news? Each of the passages in this dual passage is shorter than one full-length passage, AND the questions are organized for you so that you know which questions relate to which passage.

And that's all you need to get started! Try out the diagnostic exam on the following pages. After you complete it, you'll be able to determine which chapters will be the most useful for you. Give it your best shot! Knowing which concepts are difficult for you is the first step to improving, so there's no need to be perfect.

1.3 ACT Reading Diagnostic Exam

Now that you have a sense of what the ACT Reading section looks like, it's time to figure out some of your strengths and weaknesses as a reader and as a test-taker. Try reading these two passages and answering the questions. The following chapters contain strategies that will help you master the ACT Reading section in the future, but for now, just try your best. You will need a timer of some sort and a pencil.

Important! Find a quiet location where you won't be distracted. Set a stopwatch when you begin: don't rush, but complete each passage as if it were a real test. When you finish both passages and sets of questions, jot down the time on your stopwatch. This number will help determine your current pace. After you've completed the passages, answer the Qualitative Questions that ask about how you felt as you read.

Passage I

LITERARY NARRATIVE: This passage is adapted from the short story *Perception and Belief* by Paul Bertrand (©2014 by Bertrand National Press).

As a child, more fond of computers than books, of science than art, I loved her in the only way I knew: with a kind of condescension, befitting more the parent than the son. As a teenager, my condescension gave way in public to embarrassment and in private to a sullenness I felt ashamed of even then. How volatile was that mix of adolescent tenderness and anger, how confusing to brood, without motive, through those charming domestic years with my mother. I did not believe in her work, and to this day I largely don't; yet somehow I totally believed in her. The contradiction shaped our relationship, of course, though I can't have known then how hugely it would shape my own beliefs.

In the advertisements tacked to the bulletin board of our local natural grocer, she dubbed herself a "Healer," a precise term in comparison to the practice it named. My mother's specialty, as it was, encompassed the entire ouvre of medically evasive symptoms: fatigue, joint pain, back pain, headache, digestive health. If traditional medicine had failed, or worse, dismissed your claims, she could offer help. Were it not my mother smiling from the poster, or our home number listed as the contact, I might have felt her ads were predatory, exploitative. As it was, my dominant feeling was confusion: my mother's astonishing claims, it turns out, were backed up by apparent results.

Her office was in the eave above the kitchen: a converted wedge, no more, and cramped for that. As a rule, I was not allowed inside—the wedge was sanctum—but mere exclusion did not stop me, budding skeptic, from watching each client's arrival from the window in my bedroom. The clients all drove hatchbacks, which I thought was funny. As they came slinking into our driveway, like stray cats approaching some bowl of oatmeal my mother had left out on the steps, I raced from my bedroom to the kitchen, where a small vent in the ceiling allowed me to eavesdrop on the conversations above. Listening to the hushed conversation upstairs, to the chimes, to the singing—yes, singing—I nurtured seeds of frustration that, ironically, blossomed into questions, many of them at the heart of my career today. What, exactly, did she believe? What did they? How did they believe? Why? And perhaps above all, why did it all seem to work?

I had been able to see the room only once, and then as a glance through a cracked door, when my mother called me upstairs in desperation to fix her printer. Relegated with some embarrassment to a corner in a small hallway outside the room (an uneasy concession to the late twentieth century), the printer was only jammed. A simple tug on an errant sheet removed the problem from the gears. But in those fifteen seconds, I caught a glimpse through the door of shelves baroquely lined with talismans and crystals and old books—a veneer, in short, of age and knowledge. For years, it was the only glimpse I got, and I held closely to the image.

Still, to listen at the vent below (and to smell—some church-like odor emerged from its gills) was enough to be immersed in a sensory experience. It was something akin to ritual. A shared creative act between mother, client, and, unbeknownst to them, boy eavesdropping at the vent below. For the people who arrived daily in our driveway, the experience evinced a real—and I mean this in the objective sense—transformation. Likewise, for the artist weaving the experience, her subjection to the experience, and her belief in its reality, was total. My mother wove a fabric of which she herself was an integral part. I myself could not escape the grip that her work held on my life.

Yet it would be possible to overstate my acceptance of that phenomenon. There is deep, intractable conflict between my mother and me, despite, perhaps because of, the deep fondness we feel for one another. For her clients, those endurers of imprecise maladies, there may be relief in imprecise cures. But what danger lurks for those with treatable conditions who eschew proven medicine for the promise of "natural healing"? My mother's work embodies both the art and the lie, creations we must admit give life to one another. It is not my intent to engage here with the danger of the lie, but rather to investigate the promise of the art, to look through the window it affords onto human perception. My mother wove a fabric, and understood intuitively that she could construct for herself, her clients, and (unbeknownst to her) her son, an entire world. Or perhaps she did know. Perhaps, playing the artist's longest game, she knew exactly the questions she wanted me to ask.

1. The primary function of the third paragraph (lines 27–43) is to:

A. critique the narrator's mother's beliefs about nontraditional medicine.
B. correct misconceptions about the healing arts.
C. summarize the narrator's feelings about his mother's clients.
D. describe the narrator's observations of his mother's practice.

2. Based on the passage, which of the following best describes the narrator's opinion of his mother's work?

F. He completely denies his mother's abilities as a healer.
G. He believes in the experience his mother creates but is skeptical of her techniques.
H. He considers his mother to be the best example of a healer.
J. He feels guilty that he never confronted his mother's clients to suggest that they see a doctor.

3. According to the passage, the narrator's mother offered services for patients when:

A. traditional medicine did not work.
B. they could not afford a hospital stay.
C. a doctor wrote a referral for nontraditional treatment.
D. an acupuncturist was unable to improve the patient's condition.

4. The passage most strongly suggests that the experience "evinced a real...transformation" (lines 62–63) for the patients because the narrator's mother:

F. always healed the patients by the time they left.
G. was actually trained in traditional medicine.
H. had scientifically proven that her methods worked.
J. believed in her work.

5. As it is used in line 17, the word *encompassed* most nearly means:

A. surrounded.
B. included.
C. caused.
D. held within.

6. The narrator states that his mother's title of Healer was:

F. only given after years of practice.
G. given to her by a local grocer.
H. more precise than the job it described.
J. less precise than the job it described.

7. The tone of this passage can be best described as:

A. analytical and contemplative.
B. irate yet sympathetic.
C. argumentative and spiteful.
D. objective and blunt.

8. The main idea of the fourth paragraph (lines 44–55) is that:

F. technologies within the narrator's mother's office were outdated.
G. the narrator's mother lacked the skills necessary to fix the printer.
H. the clutter within the office bothered the narrator.
J. the narrator eagerly took advantage of any opportunity to see the office.

9. The narrator mentions all of the following as maladies of his mother's patients EXCEPT:

A. predatory disposition.
B. digestive issues.
C. back pain.
D. fatigue.

10. The author most likely includes the sentence in lines 72–74 in order to:

F. reveal his ultimate conclusion about the validity of his mother's occupation.
G. contradict those who would question the work of healers.
H. concede a point before questioning its worth in some circumstances.
J. demonstrate the narrator's unwavering support of his mother.

Passage IV

NATURAL SCIENCE: This passage is adapted from the article "Acquisition of Language" by Forrest Whitmore (©2016 by Whitmore Sciences).

One of the enduring mysteries of human learning can be observed across all cultures: adults struggle to learn new languages while infants acquire their parents' native language seemingly without effort. Similarly, while children exposed to multiple languages achieve bilingual (or even trilingual) fluency, adolescents and adults almost always struggle with fluency, particularly in areas of pronunciation. The distinctions are linked to age, but the precise mechanism that makes language acquisition different for children and adults remains elusive. In an effort to better understand how language is acquired, scientists have turned to both human studies and biological analogy for explanatory evidence; increasingly, findings suggest that differences in language acquisition are linked to changes in the developing brain.

Many studies have focused on the most widely held theory of language acquisition: the Critical Period Hypothesis. The theory posits that the time frame for language acquisition is biologically constrained by age. For humans, the critical period seems to correspond roughly with the years from birth to the onset of puberty, at which point the ability to learn new languages rapidly declines. The correlation between declining language acquisition and the onset of puberty suggests that a biological or neurological mechanism determines the critical period's time frame.

Various explanations exist for what this neurological mechanism may be: some research suggests that changes in the hippocampus—the brain's center for memory, learning, and emotion—result in a relative attrition of procedural memory, the neurological ability to unconsciously link ideas together into a repeatable act that many researchers believe is foundational to language acquisition. Differences in procedural memory could help explain why native speakers and children learning new languages work subconsciously, while non-native adult learners rely almost entirely on declarative memory, consciously linking together remembered vocabulary words in consciously created grammatical constructions.

Additional evidence that the Critical Period Hypothesis may be correct can be found in analogies between the language acquisition of humans and that of other species. Some of the most compelling research has focused on the critical period in birds, during which time they learn species-specific songs critical to mate attraction and territorial claims. Researchers have consistently found that, across species, birds learn and practice only the calls to which they were exposed in their first months after hatching. Months, and even years later, regardless of additional exposure to diverse songs of other species, birds practice only the songs originally acquired in the first one to two months in the nest. What's more, birds exposed to the calls of multiple species in their first months after hatching show a clear preference for the songs of their own species, thus suggesting an instinctive—that is, a biological—underpinning for even the recognition of particular sounds. Fluency, it seems, in both birds and humans, may be constrained by biological time.

By making a compelling analogy between birds' preference for particular bird sounds and the human preference for particular phonemes (the distinct units of sound that vary widely from language to language) researchers are bettering their understanding of how humans acquire spoken language fluency. In humans, linguistic phonemes allow speakers and listeners to construct and hear different words. In English, for instance, the sounds for "r" and "l" are distinct phonemes, easily distinguished by native speakers, but those sounds are not apparent to all humans who were not exposed to English during the critical period of language acquisition. Unlike recently-hatched birds, human infants show no particular preference for any set of phonemes and acquire sounds with equal proclivity.

Research into human language acquisition and analogous animal vocalization acquisition has demonstrated that, to some large extent, both language and vocalization are linked to the structure and growth of the brain. While the sounds that various species articulate must be learned, that can only happen by tapping into biologically-determined neurological systems that make the environmental input possible. Further research will seek to better understand the precise mechanisms at work in language acquisition. Perhaps with new educational methods and interventions that take advantage of advantages in neurological and biological science, it will be possible to better pinpoint a concrete explanation.

11. The main idea of the passage is that:

A. adults attempting to learn a new language will never be able to have the same fluency as children who learned the language from their parents.
B. birds and humans acquire language in nearly identical ways.
C. research suggests that language acquisition happens most fluently in the beginning of a human's life.
D. the "critical period" is the only time in which humans can acquire language.

12. According to the passage, birds typically learn fluent calls:

F. by instinct, without the need to learn from birds of the same species.
G. in order to attract the strongest mates from a variety of species.
H. only when exposed to those particular calls by a certain age.
J. from birds of other species in their immediate area.

13. The primary purpose of the fourth paragraph (lines 40–58) is to:

A. explain how language acquisition is similar in both birds' and humans' abilities to distinguish between particular sounds during their "critical period."
B. argue that babies do not inherently demonstrate a preference for any one language.
C. conclude the author's argument by emphatically stating that adults cannot acquire language in the same manner as babies can.
D. dispute research that phonemes specific to a given language cannot be distinguished if humans acquire the language in later years.

14. The author's tone can be best described as:

F. ambivalent.
G. analytical.
H. antagonistic.
J. admiring.

15. The author most likely includes the parenthetical statement in lines 61–62 in order to:

A. explain how specific sounds can only be distinguished by native language speakers.
B. provide an example of how languages are fundamentally similar.
C. demonstrate how humans and birds have similar foundational language units.
D. clarify a specialized vocabulary term that readers may be unfamiliar with.

16. The passage mostly strongly suggests that the neurological feature that provides support for the Critical Period Hypothesis is:

F. phonemes.
G. the prefrontal cortex.
H. the hippocampus.
J. neuroplasticity.

17. According to lines 34–39, as humans age, the mechanisms used to learn language:

A. shift to memory that requires conscious thought.
B. allow for the ability to assimilate language into procedural memory.
C. become completely independent of assimilation abilities.
D. remain at a consistent level.

18. The main idea of the fifth paragraph (lines 59–73) is that:

F. the study of bird sound acquisition allows scientists to better understand human langauge acquisition.
G. baby birds demonstrate a clear preference for both songs of their own species and for songs that they heard while still in the nest.
H. humans and birds have similar early timeframes for optimal language acquisition.
J. abandoned birds who don't have exposure to their species' song grow up unable to attract mates.

19. As it is used in lines 10–11, the word *elusive* most nearly means:

A. slippery.
B. uncaring.
C. immaterial.
D. unknown.

20. The author states that puberty is related to language acquisition because:

F. after puberty, humans can no longer process language.
G. before puberty, humans can acquire language without conscious effort.
H. before puberty, humans can learn language only through explicit teaching.
J. after puberty, humans take in language despite the fact that the brain is fully formed.

STOP YOUR STOPWATCH. Congratulations on finishing two ACT Reading passages! You've taken the first step to help you learn how to beat the ACT at its own game.

Qualitative Questions

21. Did you find yourself reading the same thing over and over without understanding what it was saying? Yes // No

22. Did you find it challenging to focus or to know what to focus on? Yes // No

23. Did you complete the two passages in 18 minutes or less?[1] Yes // No

24. Did you think you understood the passages overall, but you struggled with the questions? Yes // No

25. Did you find one passage significantly more challenging than the other? Yes // No

[1]Do you have timing accommodations? If so, go to page 151.

Answer Key

Question	Answer	Reading Comp	Specific Detail	Purpose
1.	D			________
2.	G	________		
3.	A		________	
4.	J		________	
5.	B		________	
6.	H		________	
7.	A	________		
8.	J	________		
9.	A		________	
10.	H			________
11.	C	________		
12.	H		________	
13.	A			________
14.	G	________		
15.	D			________
16.	H		________	
17.	A		________	
18.	F	________		
19.	D		________	
20.	G		________	
Total	________	________	________	________

How to use this book... The best way to work through this book is from beginning to end. Of course, not everyone has time for that. If you're taking the ACT soon, the following table will help you direct your focus to the sections that will be most helpful to you.

Diagnostic Exam				
	Your Score	**If your score is between...**	**You may have found it challenging to...**	**Then work through...**
Reading Comp		0–4	Understand *what* the passage is talking about	• Chapter 2 (p. 19) • Chapter 3: Main Idea (p. 51)
Specific Detail		0–7	Understand *how* to find the precise information	• Chapter 3: Specific Detail (p. 45)
Purpose		0-3	Understand *why* certain information is in the passage	• Chapter 3: Purpose (p. 53)
Qualitative Questions				
	Yes	**No**		**If yes, work through...**
21.				• Chapter 2: Annotation Strategies (p. 20)
22.				• Chapter 2: Annotation Strategies (p. 20)
23.				• Chapter 4 (p. 71)
24.				• Chapter 3 (p. 43)
25.				• Chapter 4: Reordering the Passages (p. 72)

1.4 Your Study Timeline

Use the following table to plan how you are going to use this book. Having a structured study plan can be a really helpful way to stay in control of this process.

<table>
<tr><th></th><th>To Do</th><th>Due Date</th><th>What you'll learn...</th><th>Done!</th></tr>
<tr><td>Chapter 1</td><td>X</td><td>Today!</td><td>A basic overview of what you can expect to see on the ACT Reading section!</td><td>X</td></tr>
<tr><td>Chapter 2</td><td></td><td></td><td>• Annotating the Text
• Textual Mapping
• Theme and Tone
• Critical Reading of Questions</td><td></td></tr>
<tr><td>Chapter 3</td><td></td><td></td><td>Types of ACT Questions
• Specific Detail
• Main Idea
• Purpose</td><td></td></tr>
<tr><td>Chapter 4</td><td>X</td><td></td><td>Chapter 4 contains strategies that are useful to everyone!
• Reordering Passages
• The Read
• Timing
• Reordering Questions
• Process of Elimination
• Guessing Strategies</td><td></td></tr>
<tr><td>Practice Test 1</td><td></td><td></td><td></td><td></td></tr>
<tr><td>Practice Test 2</td><td></td><td></td><td></td><td></td></tr>
<tr><td>Practice Test 3</td><td></td><td></td><td></td><td></td></tr>
</table>

Chapter 2

Reading Comprehension

Key Topics
- Annotating the Text
- Textual Mapping
- Theme
- Tone
- Critical Reading of Questions and Answer Choices

The passages that the ACT Reading section asks you to read can sometimes be complex. Here is an example introductory paragraph:

> **SOCIAL SCIENCE** This passage is adapted from *The Literacy Curve* by Lauren Hastings (©2017 by Hastings Inc.).
>
> " the ascendance of digital media (from video to music streaming to social media to podcasts to video games), a once-simmering panic in academia is now overboiling, as many educators, long wary of American literacy's slow decline, now believe reading as we know it may actually be dying. Research suggests the fear is not unfounded—by some measures Americans are reading less and lower quality material than ever before. But is the situation truly dire? The current state of reading in America is complicated, in some ways more promising, but in other ways even worse than the most pessimistic critics suggest."

Don't worry if you find this paragraph confusing—this chapter will help you break down even the most challenging passages.

What actually *is* reading comprehension?

Reading comprehension is about the act of reading itself: not timing, not answering questions, just understanding the passage. Focused reading helps identify the **theme** and **tone** of ACT Reading passages.

Why is it so important? ↳ more on both later in this chapter!

If you can identify the **theme** and **tone** of a passage, you can answer many ACT Reading questions.

How do I find theme and tone?

Here are two essential strategies for identifying theme and tone: annotating the passage and textual mapping. Keep reading to learn these skills!

2.1 Annotating the Passage

What is annotating?
Annotating is the act of underlining and circling as you read. It helps you to...

- Focus on key information
- Follow the thread of the author's argument
- Engage with the passage from beginning to end

How do I know what to annotate?
The ACT follows common patterns, so you can be on the lookout for the same passage details test after test. Here are the five key details to look for as you read. They will often point to the answers to ACT Reading questions. To help you remember the annotations, there's a convenient acronym: **CLOSE** (think CLOSE reading). Take a look at these examples from the paragraph on p. 19.

- Chronology: Time words help you keep track of when key events are taking place.

  > "...a once-simmering panic in academia is now overboiling..."

  There is a time shift. The phrase "once-simmering" suggests the situation used to be "simmering." Then something changed over time: "now" the situation is "overboiling."

  > "Research suggests the fear is not unfounded—by some measures Americans are reading less and lower quality material than ever before. But is the situation truly dire?"

  The phrase "than ever before" again indicates that a change is happening over time. Americans are reading different material now. The time words in this sentence suggest that the state of reading is an ongoing issue, one that continues to change even now.

- Lists/Repetition: Lists use specific examples to indicate the importance of particular ideas. Repetition, either in one paragraph or throughout the passage, suggests a word or idea is important to the main idea.

  > "Provoked by the ascendance of digital media (from video and music streaming to social media to podcasts to video games), a once-simmering panic in academia is now overboiling, as many educators, wary of American literacy's slow decline, now believe reading as we know it may actually be doomed."

  The list in parentheses provides examples of an important subject in the passage: digital media. The repetition of the word "now" demonstrates the sense of urgency that educators feel.

- Opposition/Contrast: Contrast words and phrases are always important. They mark key points and shifts in the author's argument.

  > "Research suggests the fear is not unfounded—by some measures Americans are reading less and lower quality material than ever before. But is the situation truly dire?"

  > "The current state of reading in America is complex, in some ways better, but in other ways even worse than the most pessimistic critics suggest."

  The contrast words suggest a central theme: an ongoing debate about the positives and the negatives of American literacy.

- Specialized Language: Look for words—hypotheses, theories, technical terms—that are specific to a topic. Specialized language also includes figurative language (think similes and metaphors), which can be particularly prominent in fiction passages.

> "Provoked by the ascendance of digital media (from video and music streaming to social media to podcasts to video games), a once-simmering panic in academia is now overboiling, as many educators, wary of American literacy's slow decline, now believe reading as we know it may actually be doomed."

Here, "digital media" acts as a technical term that is defined in the parentheses. "Once-simmering" and "overboiling" both work as figurative language. They hint at a sense of urgency or anxiety associated with the subject.

- Emotional Language/Opinion: It's important to be conscious of how authors or people in a passage feel. Emotional language can indicate how the narrator feels about the topic being discussed, or it can reveal how characters feel about each other.

> "...many educators, long wary of American literacy's slow decline, now believe reading as we know it may actually be doomed."

The transition from "wary" to "doomed" suggests that educators are feeling worse and worse about the decline in reading skills.

Set up an annotation key and stick to it! That way, when you scan your annotated passage, you'll know what each symbol stands for. For example...

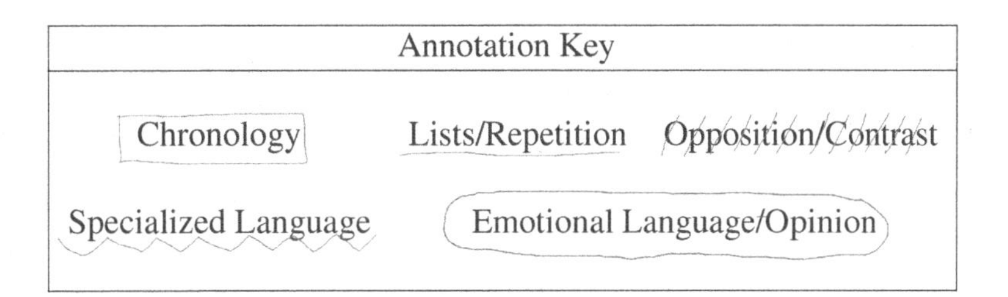

When should I annotate the passage?

When you're taking the ACT Reading section, you should always be moving your pencil. Think of it as an extension of your brain, helping to focus attention and to clarify critical thinking with lines and circles and notes. That said, CLOSE proves especially helpful for the following scenarios:

- **As you read the passage:** If the passage is challenging to understand, or if you have a hard time focusing, annotate the passage as you read.
- **As you answer the questions:** If you already feel comfortable understanding the passages, annotate when you go back to the passage to help locate answers to the questions.
- **All the time:** When you're first starting to use CLOSE, it's a good idea to practice annotating whenever you read something.

Try it! Annotate the passage on the following page. The first paragraph has been completed to get you started!

Passage II

SOCIAL SCIENCE: This passage is adapted from *The Literacy Curve* by Lauren Hastings (©2017 by Hastings Inc.).

Provoked by the ascendance of digital media (from video to music streaming to social media to podcasts to video games), a once-simmering panic in academia is now overboiling, as many educators, long wary of American literacy's slow decline, now believe reading as we know it may actually be dying. Research suggests their fear is not unfounded—by some measures Americans are reading less and lower quality material than ever before. But is the situation truly dire? The current state of reading in America is complicated, in some ways more promising, but in other ways even worse than the most pessimistic critics suggest.

For the most apocalyptic thinkers, panicked we are entering a new Stone Age of literacy, history might offer an important, and grounding, corrective. Until the turn of the 20th century, illiteracy was the norm, and even for the literate few in the early 1900s, the quality of reading material was poor. Partisan journalism and low quality books were by far the most popular texts. There can be a tendency to romanticize the past, and to compare a general public that once read Dickens to one that now reads Twitter. But Dickens stands out precisely because he was the exception to the rule: the rare great writer who was actually popular.

The fact is, the general public has rarely been very good at reading—either deeply or widely. George Orwell, for example, famously complained in 1940 that because the international public read mostly cheap sentimental stories and "boys' magazines," ignorance of great literature and world events was inevitable. In the 1950s in America, Ray Bradbury published his dystopian novel *Fahrenheit 451*, which in part mourned the death of the book by television. Fear of literacy's decline has been, in other words, around a long time.

The good news is that reading rates increase steadily with education and income, and America today is richer and better-educated than ever before. Higher education in America continues to grow rapidly, and if the trend continues, there is reason to believe that literacy in America will soon achieve, by some measures, a new high point. Over 90% of college graduates report having read at least one book in the past year.

But other metrics indicate cause for the same concerns that worried previous generations. Today's public may be more literate generally, but basic literacy does not necessarily entail advanced reading or critical thinking. By these measures, Americans may actually be declining from heights achieved in the mid 20th century, a golden period of reading sandwiched between great improvements in general education and the rise of video and the Internet. Since the late 1970s, for example, the percentage of the public that is able to, but does not, read, nearly tripled from 8% to 23%. That's one quarter of literate Americans who have read not one book in the entire past year. Among those who do read, the median number of books read per year is only 5, down from 9 in the 1970s. Perhaps of most concern, 30% of adults are reading at only a basic level according to national education standards.

The reading habits of young adults are similarly concerning. Evidence suggests that the current generation of 18–24 year olds reads more words than any prior generation, but in shorter, simpler, more predictable excerpts. An overwhelming amount of all their total reading is in the form of news articles and social media posts, almost entirely nonfiction or simpler non-literary forms. There may be real cognitive skills associated with reading and processing ever-increasing bits of information, but the skills have little to do with the close reading or sustained critical thinking that long-form reading demands. Many social media posts, for instance, can be read in less than 30 seconds. A full grasp of their meaning from beginning to end requires no sustained attention or assessment of various viewpoints. Similarly, information disseminated in memes and excerpts is easily digested and requires little analysis. In a world of summaries and excerpts, close reading withers. Deep reading is more than an act of consumption; it requires careful attention to the precise meanings of words, the parsing of sentences, and an ability to distinguish between similar, but subtly different, ideas.

Thus the problem, while not absolute, seems clear. Literacy has grown broad, but shallow. The first step to improving true literacy is to recognize the irreplaceable value of books and long-form works of sustained writing. Short articles and social media posts may offer rapid communication and dissemination of fact, but great essays offer far more than facts, and great literature far more than a series of events or succession of easy-to-identify themes. Writing is an exploration of ideas, character, and philosophy, rich in imagery and ideas from sentence to sentence. True reading must engage at a deeper level.

2.2 Textual Mapping

What is textual mapping?
A textual map helps you to identify the main idea of each paragraph. The main ideas are like a "map" you can use to find answers more quickly. The textual map also reveals the structure of the passage.

Why should I map the text?
The visual guide created by a textual map helps you in three ways:

- Helps you track the theme
- Helps you locate key details
- Helps you see the structure of the passage at a glance (sometimes, ACT Reading questions even directly ask about the structure of the passage)

How do I create a map of the text?
For each paragraph, identify the Who/What/Where. *Who* are the main players? *What* are the key concepts? *Where* is this taking place?

Then, in the margins, write one word or a short phrase that summarizes what you've found in each paragraph. This will not only help you to find answers when the time comes, but it will also help to follow the author's story or main idea as you read.

Make sure to note major shifts that take place in the text. These could be changes in the argument, the author's tone, or the setting or time period. (You can annotate major shifts by paying attention to the O in CLOSE.)

"Provoked by the ascendance of digital media (from video to music streaming to social media to podcasts to video games), a once-simmering panic in academia is now overboiling, as many educators, long wary of American literacy's slow decline, now believe reading as we know it may actually be dying. Research suggests their fear is not unfounded—by some measures Americans are reading less and lower quality material than ever before. But is the situation truly dire? The current state of reading in America is complicated, in some ways more promising, but in other ways even worse than the most pessimistic critics suggest."

Try it! On the following page, write in the main idea of each paragraph to create a textual map. This copy is annotated to act as an answer key for your previous work, but remember that you don't need to annotate absolutely everything! The goal is comprehension, so you're good to go as long as you're understanding the text.

Passage II

SOCIAL SCIENCE: This passage is adapted from *The Literacy Curve* by Lauren Hastings (©2017 by Hastings Inc.).

Provoked by the ascendance of digital media (from video to music streaming to social media to podcasts to video games), a once-simmering panic in academia is now overboiling, as many educators, long wary of American literacy's slow decline, now believe reading as we know it may actually be dying. Research suggests their fear is not unfounded—by some measures Americans are reading less and lower quality material than ever before. But is the situation truly dire? The current state of reading in America is complicated, in some ways more promising, but in other ways even worse than the most pessimistic critics suggest.

For the most apocalyptic thinkers, panicked we are entering a new Stone Age of literacy, history might offer an important, and grounding, corrective. Until the turn of the 20th century, illiteracy was the norm, and even for the literate few in the early 1900s, the quality of reading material was poor. Partisan journalism and low quality books were by far the most popular texts. There can be a tendency to romanticize the past, and to compare a general public that once read Dickens to one that now reads Twitter. But Dickens stands out precisely because he was the exception to the rule: the rare great writer who was actually popular.

The fact is, the general public has rarely been very good at reading—either deeply or widely. George Orwell, for example, famously complained in 1940 that because the international public read mostly cheap sentimental stories and "boys' magazines," ignorance of great literature and world events was inevitable. In the 1950s in America, Ray Bradbury published his dystopian novel *Fahrenheit 451*, which in part mourned the death of the book by television. Fear of literacy's decline has been, in other words, around a long time.

The good news is that reading rates increase steadily with education and income, and America today is richer and better-educated than ever before. Higher education in America continues to grow rapidly, and if the trend continues, there is reason to believe that literacy in America will soon achieve, by some measures, a new high point. Over 90% of college graduates report having read at least one book in the past year.

But other metrics indicate cause for the same concerns that worried previous generations. Today's public may be more literate generally, but basic literacy does not necessarily entail advanced reading or critical thinking. By these measures, Americans may actually be declining from heights achieved in the mid 20th century, a golden period of reading sandwiched between great improvements in general education and the rise of video and the Internet. Since the late 1970s, for example, the percentage of the public that is able to, but does not, read, nearly tripled from 8% to 23%. That's one quarter of literate Americans who have read not one book in the entire past year. Among those who do read, the median number of books read per year is only 5, down from 9 in the 1970s. Perhaps of most concern, 30% of adults are reading at only a basic level according to national education standards.

The reading habits of young adults are similarly concerning. Evidence suggests that the current generation of 18–24 year olds reads more words than any prior generation, but in shorter, simpler, more predictable excerpts. An overwhelming amount of all their total reading is in the form of news articles and social media posts, almost entirely nonfiction or simpler non-literary forms. There may be real cognitive skills associated with reading and processing ever-increasing bits of information, but the skills have little to do with the close reading or sustained critical thinking that long-form reading demands. Many social media posts, for instance, can be read in less than 30 seconds. A full grasp of their meaning from beginning to end requires no sustained attention or assessment of various viewpoints. Similarly, information disseminated in memes and excerpts is easily digested and requires little analysis. In a world of summaries and excerpts, close reading withers. Deep reading is more than an act of consumption; it requires careful attention to the precise meanings of words, the parsing of sentences, and an ability to distinguish between similar, but subtly different, ideas.

Thus the problem, while not absolute, seems clear. Literacy has grown broad, but shallow. The first step to improving true literacy is to recognize the irreplaceable value of books and long-form works of sustained writing. Short articles and social media posts may offer rapid communication and dissemination of fact, but great essays offer far more than facts, and great literature far more than a series of events or succession of easy-to-identify themes. Writing is an exploration of ideas, character, and philosophy, rich in imagery and ideas from sentence to sentence. True reading must engage at a deeper level.

Answer Key: Again, remember that your textual map does NOT need to exactly mirror this one. As long as you understand the Who/What/Where of each paragraph, you're all set!

Passage II

SOCIAL SCIENCE: This passage is adapted from *The Literacy Curve* by Lauren Hastings (©2017 by Hastings Inc.).

Provoked by the ascendance of digital media (from video to music streaming to social media to podcasts to video games), a once-simmering panic in academia is now overboiling, as many educators, long wary of American literacy's slow decline, now believe reading as we know it may actually be dying. Research suggests their fear is not unfounded—by some measures Americans are reading less and lower quality material than ever before. But is the situation truly dire? The current state of reading in America is complicated, in some ways more promising, but in other ways even worse than the most pessimistic critics suggest.

For the most apocalyptic thinkers, panicked we are entering a new Stone Age of literacy, history might offer an important, and grounding, corrective. Until the turn of the 20th century, illiteracy was the norm, and even for the literate few in the early 1900s, the quality of reading material was poor. Partisan journalism and low-quality books were by far the most popular texts. There can be a tendency to romanticize the past, and to compare a general public that once read Dickens to one that now reads Twitter. But Dickens stands out precisely because he was the exception to the rule: the rare great writer who was actually popular.

The fact is, the general public has rarely been very good at reading—either deeply or widely. George Orwell, for example, famously complained in 1940 that because the international public read mostly cheap sentimental stories and "boys' magazines," ignorance of great literature and world events was inevitable. In the 1950s in America, Ray Bradbury published his dystopian novel *Fahrenheit 451*, which in part mourned the death of the book by television. Fear of literacy's decline has been, in other words, around a long time.

The good news is that reading rates increase steadily with education and income, and America today is richer and better-educated than ever before. Higher education in America continues to grow rapidly, and if the trend continues, there is reason to believe that literacy in America will soon achieve, by some measures, a new high point. Over 90% of college graduates report having read at least one book in the past year.

But other metrics indicate cause for the same concerns that worried previous generations. Today's public may be more literate generally, but basic literacy does not necessarily entail advanced reading or critical thinking. By these measures, Americans may actually be declining from heights achieved in the mid 20th century, a golden period of reading sandwiched between great improvements in general education and the rise of video and the Internet. Since the late 1970s, for example, the percentage of the public that is able to, but does not, read, nearly tripled from 8% to 23%. That's one quarter of literate Americans who have read not one book in the entire past year. Among those who do read, the median number of books read per year is only 5, down from 9 in the 1970s. Perhaps of most concern, 30% of adults are reading at only a basic level according to national education standards.

The reading habits of young adults are similarly concerning. Evidence suggests that the current generation of 18–24 year olds reads more words than any prior generation, but in shorter, simpler, more predictable excerpts. An overwhelming amount of all their total reading is in the form of news articles and social media posts, almost entirely nonfiction or simpler non-literary forms. There may be real cognitive skills associated with reading and processing ever-increasing bits of information, but the skills have little to do with the close reading or sustained critical thinking that long-form reading demands. Many social media posts, for instance, can be read in less than 30 seconds. A full grasp of their meaning from beginning to end requires no sustained attention or assessment of various viewpoints. Similarly, information disseminated in memes and excerpts is easily digested and requires little analysis. In a world of summaries and excerpts, close reading withers. Deep reading is more than an act of consumption; it requires careful attention to the precise meanings of words, the parsing of sentences, and an ability to distinguish between similar, but subtly different, ideas.

Thus the problem, while not absolute, seems clear. Literacy has grown broad, but shallow. The first step to improving true literacy is to recognize the irreplaceable value of books and long-form works of sustained writing. Short articles and social media posts may offer rapid communication and dissemination of fact, but great essays offer far more than facts, and great literature far more than a series of events or succession of easy-to-identify themes. Writing is an exploration of ideas, character, and philosophy, rich in imagery and ideas from sentence to sentence. True reading must engage at a deeper level.

2.3 Theme

Okay, we've put it off long enough. It's now time to talk about theme and tone!

What, exactly, is theme?
Theme is more than just the topic of a passage; it's also the author's specific take on that topic. Keep in mind: every ACT Reading passage was written by a real author for a real reason. Your goal is to find that reason.

Theme can be illustrated by the following formula:

topic + argument = theme

Topic is what the passage is about. The title of the passage can sometimes give an indication of the topic.

Argument is what the author thinks about that topic.

Here are some examples :

Topic	Argument	Theme
War	not essential for societies to improve	War is not essential for societies to improve.
Rabbits	invasive species that should be contained	The rabbit is an invasive species that should be contained.

So how do I find the theme?

Short Answer: Look in the conclusion! The last paragraph of ACT Reading passages is essential reading. In conclusions, authors make their final claims—therefore, the conclusions often summarize the theme of an entire passage.

Long Answer: Introductions are good, too. And so are topic sentences. Putting these all together, you can find the theme of any ACT Reading passage by looking at the following:

- The first paragraph, which introduces the topic
- The topic sentences, which indicate the key components of the author's argument
- The last paragraph, which wraps up the central argument

The following exercise will illustrate how to find the theme for any ACT Reading passage, an absolutely essential skill for improving your score. First, read and annotate the short passage below.

Passage I

LITERARY NARRATIVE: This passage is adapted from the short story *This is a Fake Story About the ACT* by The tutor who wrote this book. (©3020 by Fake Press).

"The ACT is my favorite!" she said, and looked like she actually believed it. The performance fleece, the light-up watch, the hair tightly cinched with a pink rubber band—it all said, "I take tests for fun."

5 In fact, the tutor was by all appearances exactly like every other teacher in Mallory's life: evolved to exist precisely in one room, in one clearly-defined parameter of time, endlessly teaching in one particular ecosystem of a subject, or in this case, test. It was no more possible 10 to imagine the tutor's exterior existence than it was to believe history teachers went grocery shopping, or to believe that Mrs. Hastings had a husband with whom she went to dinner.

Yet the tutor was good. Or she seemed it. For one, 15 she was not always saying empty, terrible things to make Mallory feel better, as other adults in Mallory's life had done. The worst thing Mallory's father ever said was, "Do you know what ACT stands for? A Cool Test." This while throwing at her the test that stood between Mallory 20 and every dream she had for a life after high school.

It's true that the tutor, too, was a perpetrator of acronym. But the tutor's ideas were precise, without gimmick, and by the time they entered the reading section of the test, Mallory was beginning to believe some very 25 strange ideas. Like the book of exams between them—all five pounds of it—was not a wall separating this lousy town from Mallory's quad-side dorm, but was instead "a gateway" through which to enter it. And though it's true the tutor did not say gateway "to enter it," but rather, "to 30 opportunity," Mallory was nevertheless able to see the point. As the tutor's red pen marked circles and squiggles through the heart of a passage, the marks became an incantation: the ACT is a puzzle. Puzzles can be unlocked. Unlocked puzzles reveal great secrets.

35 Could this be the beginning of a beautiful friendship? Mallory and what's-her-name? Perhaps. But first, Mallory and the ACT.

What is the *topic*?
Mallory and her new ACT tutor.

+

Argument

What's the main idea of the intro?
Mallory has a cheesy new ACT
tutor who actually likes the test.

+

What's the main idea of the conclusion?
Mallory has changed her mind about the ACT;
she might grow to like it after all.

Now just put it together:

Topic + Argument = Theme
Mallory's new ACT tutor is cheesy but effective; she helps Mallory to feel
more optimistic about taking the ACT.

Don't Forget: CLOSE. The O (opposition/contrast) in CLOSE is especially helpful when it comes to theme. Why? Contrast words—however, but, although—often point to the main arguments of a passage.

Try it! Reread your textual mapping from the *The Literacy Curve* passage and practice writing a theme by identifying the topic and the argument.

Title: ____________________

+

Topic: ____________________

____

+

Argument from...

Main Idea of Intro Paragraph: ____________________

____

+

Main Idea of Conclusion: ____________________

____

=

Theme: ____________________

____

Answer Key: Here are some possible answers for the theme of the passage. Again, it's OK if your theme doesn't match the answer key's word for word.

Title: The Literacy Curve

+

Topic: Literacy today

+

Argument from...

Main Idea of Intro Paragraph: complex state of literacy today

+

Main Idea of Conclusion: readers today need to analyze longer texts

=

Theme: Even though more people than ever read, they need to read longer, more complex texts to improve their true literacy.

2.4 Tone

What is tone? The tone is how the author feels about a subject. It is a distinct emotion.

How do I figure out the tone?

- Use the (E)motional Language/Opinion words that you circled when you annotated in your CLOSE read.
- Look at the introduction, where authors often "set the tone."
- Look at the conclusion, where authors often use strong tone to reinforce their argument.

In the example passage about Mallory, the author sets the tone in the introduction with humorous phrases such as "she actually believed it." The conclusion is similarly comical, as we find out that a friendship might form between Mallory and her tutor, but more likely it will form between Mallory and the ACT.

So, the **tone** of this passage is humorous.

Don't Forget: "Neutral" is a tone! Often, Social Science and Natural Science passages are written in the style of newspapers or textbooks. Authors of such passages actively avoid showing any bias toward their topic, so it becomes *especially important* if the authors of Social Science or Natural Science passages break from a neutral tone and reveal their feeling or opinion.

It is always helpful to begin by identifying a tone as negative, neutral, or positive. It can also be helpful to identify a more nuanced tone based on the specifics of a given passage. The table below identifies some common tones found on the ACT.

Negative	**Neutral**	**Positive**
Abrasive	Calm	Admiring
Angry	Indifferent	Enthusiastic
Anxious	Objective	Humorous
Argumentative	Serious	Optimistic
Cold	Thoughtful	Proud
Critical	Academic	Reverent
Doubtful	Analytical	Excited
Nervous	Scientific	Impressed
Pessimistic		

Try It! Look through your annotations from the sample passage *The Literacy Curve* for (E)motion to determine how the author feels about the topic. You can also look at the introduction and conclusion paragraphs.

The author's tone is ____.

Answer: Words like *wary, concerning, and curiosity* suggest that the tone is **serious yet optimistic**.

2.5 Critical Reading of Questions and Answer Choices

Wait! I thought I only needed to use reading comprehension on the passage.
Not true. Closely reading the questions and answer choices is *just* as crucial as closely reading the passages themselves.

What should I look for when reading the questions and answer choices?
Here are three key elements to watch for when reading questions and answer choices on the ACT. Close reading will keep you from falling into any ACT traps.

- **Verbs:** Pay close attention to action words, especially those found in answer choices. The verbs will help you immediately avoid incorrect answers. When you see a verb in an answer, ask yourself, "is that really what they were doing?"

  1. The main purpose of the second paragraph is to:

  A. **argue** that Mallory's tutor is a poor fit for her class.
  B. **contradict** the assertion that Mallory's tutor is similar to other adults she has encountered.
  C. **compare** similarities between Mallory's tutor and other educators.
  D. **foreshadow** Mallory's success with ACT homework

- Paragraph 2 *describes* the tutor, right?

  - Answer choice A's use of "argue" is wrong because arguing is vastly different from describing.
  - Answer choice B's use of "contradict" is wrong because the paragraph does not contain many examples of contrast.
  - Answer choice C's use of "compare" looks good. Words like "than" and "like" show comparison. This is the correct answer!
  - Answer choice D uses "foreshadow," but this paragraph does not contain many time words.

- **Nouns:** Sometimes, ACT answer choices *almost* say the exact thing you want them to say. In the world of standardized tests, however, almost correct is incorrect! To avoid choosing an almost correct answer, investigate the nouns.

  1. The main purpose of the second paragraph is to:

  A. argue that Mallory's **tutor** is a poor **fit** for her **class.**
  B. contradict the assertion that Mallory's **tutor** is similar to **other adults** she has encountered.
  C. compare similarities between Mallory's **tutor** and **other educators.**
  D. foreshadow Mallory's **success** with **ACT homework.**

- This paragraph probably doesn't focus on Mallory's "class," "adults," "educators," and "homework" all at once. Read the paragraph to find which subjects it actually contains.

  - Answer choice A has one correct noun: "Mallory's tutor." But does the paragraph say anything about Mallory's tutor being an "ill fit"? Does the paragraph discuss a "class"?
  - Answer choice B looks pretty good at first because it also has the right noun, "Mallory's tutor." And the answer correctly identifies that the paragraph makes a comparison: the tutor is similar to certain other people. But does the paragraph compare the tutor to "other adults"?
  - Answer choice C is correct. It identifies both nouns of the paragraph: "Mallory's tutor" and "other educators."
  - Answer choice D mentions two nouns: "success" and "ACT homework." But these nouns do not connect to the subjects discussed in the paragraph. The paragraph does not mention homework or success.

this word is extreme!

- **Extremes:** Extreme words in questions and answer choices *completely* restrict the meaning of what is written. For example, describing *an* embarrassing moment is completely different from describing your *most* embarrassing moment. Circle extreme words in questions and answers to keep yourself on track.
  - Which words count as extreme? Here's a word bank to get you started...
    * always/never, all/no, most/least, words ending in -est

2. Which of the following most accurately characterizes Mallory's relationship with her tutor?

F. Mallory believes her tutor is **extremely confusing**, an impression that is confirmed as the lesson continues.
G. Mallory **loves** her new tutor because of the tutor's effective test strategies and teaching method.
H. Mallory is initially somewhat suspicious of her tutor, but develops a degree of trust in the tutor's teaching method.
J. Mallory is initially disinterested in her tutor, but with time grows to believe she has the **best** teaching methods.

- This question is **not** asking for an extreme, so extreme answer choices are probably incorrect.
  - In answer choice F, *extremely confusing* is too extreme.
  - The use of the word *loves* in answer choice G is too strongly positive.
  - Answer choice H looks attractive because the use of *somewhat* and *a degree* work to keep Mallory's sentiments moderate. This is the correct answer!
  - Answer choice J uses the word *best*, which is too extreme.

3. It can be reasonably inferred from the passage that one of Mallory's least favorite interactions is one in which:

A. an adult belittles a problem of hers with empty rhetoric.
B. she sees a teacher at a restaurant or store.
C. red pen marks take over a page of her work.
D. she has a quad-side dorm.

- This question is looking for an extreme: Mallory's **least** favorite interaction. Line 17 describes the "worst" thing her father had ever done, leading to answer choice **A**!

Try it! Use the passage *The Literacy Curve* as first seen on page 22 to answer the following questions. As you critically read the questions and answer choices, circle any verbs, nouns, or extremes that could make an answer choice correct or incorrect.

1. The primary function of the second paragraph (lines 13–24) is to:

A. confirm a realistic fear that people are becoming less literate over time.
B. compare reading Dickens' novels to reading Twitter's tweets in order to prove the decline of American literacy.
C. argue that a historical shift in the type of reading popular among the general public has occurred.
D. contradict an assumption that people were more well-read in the past than they are now.

2. Based on the passage, which of the following best describes the author's opinion of the pre-technological past?

F. Literacy was completely lacking during this period.
G. Individuals today tend to romanticize and misunderstand literacy during this period.
H. During this time, literacy rates were at their highest ever.
J. This period of time is never portrayed accurately in terms of its literacy.

3. According to the passage, the reading rates of Americans today are higher than in the past because:

A. higher education is growing quickly.
B. young authors are becoming more prevalent.
C. eReaders and tablets are becoming more popular.
D. more students are hiring tutors to improve their reading skills.

4. The passage most strongly suggests that the current generation of 18–24 year olds mainly reads:

F. long-form works.
G. fiction books.
H. poetry.
J. predictable excerpts.

Answer Key

1. D. In this paragraph, the author is contradicting the assumption that people are less literate now than they were in the past. He is not confirming that assumption or arguing that a dramatic change in the type of material people read has changed. Even though he does compare Dickens and Twitter, the purpose is to show an exception, rather than to prove that Americans are less literate.

2. G. This answer avoids superlatives that are too specific: the narrator does not think that literacy was completely lacking, nor that literacy rates were the highest ever, nor that they are never portrayed accurately.

3. A. Lines 37–38 state that "Higher education in America continues to grow rapidly." The passage does not mention authors' ages, eReaders or tablets, or tutors.

4. J. Lines 61–63 state, "evidence suggests that the current generation of 18–24 year olds reads...shorter, simpler, more predictable excerpts."

2.6 Chapter Test

You've completed Chapter 2! Just to recap, you should now have a general understanding of...

- Annotating the Text
- Textual Mapping
- Theme and Tone
- Critical Reading of Questions and Answer Choices

The Chapter Test on the following pages will test these skills. Use it as an opportunity to try out everything you've learned from this chapter. That requires coordinating a lot of moving pieces, so be patient with yourself and just do your best!

CHAPTER TEST

DIRECTIONS: Read the passage and answer the questions that follow. Begin by annotating the passage (CLOSE) and creating your textual map. Write down the theme and tone. Remember to read the questions and answer choices as critically as you read the text. The following passages have been shortened, so don't worry about timing yet—you'll learn how to manage the clock in Chapter 4.

Passage I

LITERARY NARRATIVE: This passage is adapted from the short story *Summer with Alice* by Ashley Provasi. (©2014 by Literary Publishing).

I'll never forget when she sat down at the desk behind me. It was already October, the second month of school, so I was surprised to see a new kid. We had assigned seats for homeroom, of course, so she was taking 5 Alex's spot. I began to turn around to inform her of her mistake, but then I recalled my own experience changing schools in the middle of seventh grade. Adults were there to facilitate the acclimation process: I decided to let Mrs. Lupton deal with it.

10 That morning, however, Mrs. Lupton was absent, and a substitute teacher held the reins. The sub told us to sit where we wanted as long as we were quiet until the bell rang. Rookie mistake—the room was anything but quiet. It sounded like a banquet, and morning announce-15 ments passed in obscurity. I didn't even learn who the girl was until after lunch. By the time I got to fourth period, distracted by a pop quiz in Precalculus and a grueling game of dodgeball in Phys Ed, I had nearly forgotten her existence. Then, in biology, she appeared again. Mr. 20 Hehlgans stood her in front of the class and announced, "We have a new student. This is Alice, an exchange student from Sweden. Alice, would you like to introduce yourself to the class?" She just shook her head and sat in that lonely desk in the front row, the one directly in 25 front of Mr. Hehlgan's face, a chair I'd always thought of more as buffer between teacher and student than functional seat. Must be tough, I thought. Not only new, but new in another country.

As it turned out, Alice didn't talk much for the 30 first two weeks. People tried the first few days, but she seemed aloof, as if she wasn't yet ready to be a part of the swarm of Sunvale High. In the waves of gossip I caught coursing through the halls, I learned that people had decided she was egotistical. I, however, was skeptical—I 35 figured that nerves could easily be mistaken for ego, that fear of failure could be perceived as arrogance. I could see why she would find it easier to just float, to listen. One afternoon, I was getting ready for the fall lacrosse workout. As I bounced the ball against the brick wall of 40 the school, I saw Alice out of the corner of my eye. I nodded at my extra stick sitting on my bag. She picked it up, and we started to play catch—as if it were an old tradition of ours. After a few rounds, I ventured, "Have you ever played lacrosse?" To my surprise, Alice started 45 to chat. She told me that lacrosse wasn't popular in Sweden, but that she had always wanted to try. I showed her a few stick skills and asked if she wanted to join me for the team workout.

By the time spring tryouts rolled around, Alice had 50 practiced enough to make varsity. She made some friends on the team, me included, and her host family was excited to see her getting involved at school.

Looking back now on our long-term friendship, I've come to realize the importance of reaching out. Whether 55 with speech or sport, concerted efforts to find kinship among classmates can act as a bridge to human connection. Initial judgements often prove false, and an extra lacrosse stick can be the seed that grows a lifelong friendship.

Theme:

Tone:

1. The main idea of the passage is that:

A. high school students are often unkind to new arrivals.
B. lacrosse is an unpopular sport in Sweden.
C. sports can help people of different backgrounds make connections.
D. exchange students must find activities to be involved in at their new schools.

2. The tone of this passage can best be described as:

F. thoughtful and sincere.
G. condescending and disapproving.
H. irreverent and humorous.
J. whimsical and enthusiastic.

3. The third paragraph (lines 29–48) most strongly suggests that:

A. high school students are always judgmental of quiet students.
B. Alice hates being at her new school.
C. Alice only speaks Swedish and does not understand any English.
D. the narrator empathizes with Alice's nervousness.

4. The author most likely uses the description in lines 1–5 in order to:

F. illustrate the narrator's reaction to a new student.
G. contradict the information that follows in the rest of the paragraph.
H. stress Alice's negative reaction to the new school.
J. list reasons why Alice is unlikely to fit in at her new school.

5. It can most reasonably be inferred from the passage that when asked to play lacrosse, Alice feels:

A. nervous, because she has never played.
B. receptive to trying a new sport.
C. annoyed that she will have to try out for the team.
D. frustrated that other sports are not available.

Passage IV

NATURAL SCIENCE: This passage is adapted from the article "Frozen Undead: Pathogens" by Dazbog Yu. (©2014 by Bio Fundamentals Mag).

Undisturbed for over a century, a perfectly preserved human body lies frozen, layers beneath the Arctic tundra. Ice has preserved the carcass, shielding it from decay that would rot through the epidermis and soft tissue to leave only skeletal remnants. As global warming begins to thaw the otherwise impermeable ground, the scientific community flocks to discover what wonders these remains might hold. Autopsies reveal what the individual ate as a last meal and the individual's age and quality of life, among other characteristics. Most important to microbiologists, however, are the frozen pathogens—markers of disease that plagued times of yore.

In bodies that are allowed to decay, pathogens die and eventually degenerate, giving scientists limited intel into how the diseases actually functioned. When bodies are preserved by freezing, however, pathogens—like their human counterparts—become cryogenic models ripe for experimentation. By studying these preserved bodies, microbiologists can better understand diseases thought to have been completely eradicated, like smallpox. Scientists hope that this knowledge will better equip them for future deadly outbreaks.

One such scientist, Francisco Peterson of the University of Darwall, isolated a deadly strain of influenza from the soft tissue remains of a young boy, dating back to the early twentieth century, found frozen in 1997 in the Arctic Circle. He intentionally sought to revive the pathogens, slowly warming them under ideal conditions—even attempting to clone the specimens. While he was able to identify their surface proteins and genetic code, their path to reproduction—the most integral and desired information—remained elusive. His and all other attempts to revive these dead diseases have failed thus far, but that is not to say that future attempts will result in the same disappointing outcome.

Some pathogens may be more amenable to this process than others. The bacteria *Bacillus anthracis*, which causes the infection anthrax, for example, is known to burrow underground for long periods of time, only to rear its head at moments scientists cannot predict, sometimes taking out entire herds of animals. Since this pathogen has acquired evolutionary coping mechanisms that allow it to exist in this state of stasis, anthrax may actually be more easily manipulated when frozen.

Such an endeavor resembles the plot of a science fiction film grappling with the end of humanity as we know it, and it may seem odd to celebrate the rebirth of a once-extinct deadly disease. But, as Peterson describes, "The point, of course, is not to create zombie pathogens. Understanding the history and makeup of dead disease can help prevent future outbreaks."

Theme:

Tone:

6. A main theme of the passage is that:

F. cryogenic pathogens may one day be revived in a scientific lab.
G. the moral dilemma regarding the renaissance of pathogens is a difficult one.
H. contradictory opinions exist as to why pathogens should be revived.
J. pathogen reproduction could only be harmful to humans.

7. The tone of the passage can best be described as:

A. combative and contrarian.
B. informational.
C. enthusiastically optimistic.
D. abrasive.

8. The passage indicates that autopsies of frozen human remains can reveal all of the following EXCEPT:

F. the individual's general quality of life.
G. the meal the individual most often consumed.
H. pathogens responsible for the individual's death.
J. the individual's age.

9. The main purpose of the third paragraph (lines 23–35) is to:

A. contradict the notion that frozen pathogens will never be revived.
B. summarize the main argument of the passage.
C. assert that all disease revival experiments are impossible.
D. transition from a general concept to the endeavor of a specific individual.

10. The passage suggests that the most important scientific advancement regarding frozen pathogens would be:

F. information regarding how their genetic codes are similar to those of plants.
G. a multilayer mechanism to identify their surface proteins.
H. a way to identify and replicate their reproduction processes.
J. a proper way to clone them.

Answer Key

Passage I

LITERARY NARRATIVE: This passage is adapted from the short story *Summer with Alice* by Ashley Provasi. (©2014 by Literary Publishing).

I'll never forget when she sat down at the desk behind me. It was already October, the second month of school, so I was surprised to see a new kid. We had assigned seats for homeroom, of course, so she was taking Alex's spot. I began to turn around to inform her of her mistake, but then I recalled my own experience changing schools in the middle of seventh grade. Adults were there to facilitate the acclimation process: I decided to let Mrs. Lupton deal with it.

That morning, however, Mrs. Lupton was absent, and a substitute teacher held the reins. The sub told us to sit where we wanted as long as we were quiet until the bell rang. Rookie mistake—the room was anything but quiet. It sounded like a banquet, and morning announcements passed in obscurity. I didn't even learn who the girl was until after lunch. By the time I got to fourth period, distracted by a pop quiz in Precalculus and a grueling game of dodgeball in Phys Ed, I had nearly forgotten her existence. Then, in biology, she appeared again. Mr. Hehlgans stood her in front of the class and announced, "We have a new student. This is Alice, an exchange student from Sweden. Alice, would you like to introduce yourself to the class?" She just shook her head and sat in that lonely desk in the front row, the one directly in front of Mr. Hehlgan's face, a chair I'd always thought of more as buffer between teacher and student than functional seat. Must be tough, I thought. Not only new, but new in another country.

As it turned out, Alice didn't talk much for the first two weeks. People tried the first few days, but she seemed aloof, as if she wasn't yet ready to be a part of the swarm of Sunvale High. In the waves of gossip I caught coursing through the halls, I learned that people had decided she was egotistical. I, however, was skeptical—I figured that nerves could easily be mistaken for ego, that fear of failure could be perceived as arrogance. I could see why she would find it easier to just float, to listen. One afternoon, I was getting ready for the fall lacrosse workout. As I bounced the ball against the brick wall of the school, I saw Alice out of the corner of my eye. I nodded at my extra stick sitting on my bag. She picked it up, and we started to play catch—as if it were an old tradition of ours. After a few rounds, I ventured, "Have you ever played lacrosse?" To my surprise, Alice started to chat. She told me that lacrosse wasn't popular in Sweden, but that she had always wanted to try. I showed her a few stick skills and asked if she wanted to join me for the team workout.

By the time spring tryouts rolled around, Alice had practiced enough to make varsity. She made some friends on the team, me included, and her host family was excited to see her getting involved at school.

Looking back now on our long-term friendship, I've come to realize the importance of reaching out. Whether with speech or sport, concerted efforts to find kinship among classmates can act as a bridge to human connection. Initial judgements often prove false, and an extra lacrosse stick can be the seed that grows a lifelong friendship.

Title - summer with Alice + Topic - new girl at school =

Theme: Argument - The narrator befriends the new girl at school after realizing they have a lot in common

Tone: reflective, thoughtful

1. The main idea of the passage is that:
   - **A.** high school students are often unkind to new arrivals.
   - **B.** lacrosse is an unpopular sport in Sweden.
   - **C.** sports can help people of different backgrounds make connections.
   - **D.** exchange students must find activities to be involved in at their new schools.

2. The tone of this passage can best be described as:
   - **F.** thoughtful and sincere. positive
   - **G.** condescending and disapproving. negative
   - **H.** irreverent and humorous. positive & negative
   - **J.** whimsical and enthusiastic. positive

3. The third paragraph (lines 29–48) most strongly suggests that:
   - **A.** high school students are always judgmental of quiet students.
   - **B.** Alice hates being at her new school.
   - **C.** Alice only speaks Swedish and does not understand any English.
   - **D.** the narrator empathizes with Alice's nervousness.

4. The author most likely uses the description in lines 1–5 in order to:
   - **F.** illustrate the narrator's reaction to a new student.
   - **G.** contradict the information that follows in the rest of the paragraph.
   - **H.** stress Alice's negative reaction to the new school.
   - **J.** list reasons why Alice is unlikely to fit in at her new school.

5. It can most reasonably be inferred from the passage that when asked to play lacrosse, Alice feels:
   - **A.** nervous, because she has never played.
   - **B.** receptive to trying a new sport.
   - **C.** annoyed that she will have to try out for the team.
   - **D.** frustrated that other sports are not available.

Passage II

NATURAL SCIENCE: This passage is adapted from the article "Frozen Undead: Pathogens" by Dazbog Yu. (©2014 by Bio Fundamentals Mag).

Undisturbed for over a century, a perfectly preserved human body lies frozen, layers beneath the Arctic tundra. Ice has preserved the carcass, shielding it from decay that would rot through the epidermis and soft tissue to leave only skeletal remnants. As global warming begins to thaw the otherwise impermeable ground, the scientific community flocks to discover what wonders these remains might hold. Autopsies reveal what the individual ate as a last meal and the individual's age and quality of life, among other characteristics. Most important to microbiologists, however, are the frozen pathogens—markers of disease that plagued times of yore.

In bodies that are allowed to decay, pathogens die and eventually degenerate, giving scientists limited intel into how the diseases actually functioned. When bodies are preserved by freezing, however, pathogens—like their human counterparts—become cryogenic models ripe for experimentation. By studying these preserved bodies, microbiologists can better understand diseases thought to have been completely eradicated, like smallpox. Scientists hope that this knowledge will better equip them for future deadly outbreaks.

One such scientist, Francisco Peterson of the University of Darwall, isolated a deadly strain of influenza from the soft tissue remains of a young boy, dating back to the early twentieth century, found frozen in 1997 in the Arctic Circle. He intentionally sought to revive the pathogens, slowly warming them under ideal conditions—even attempting to clone the specimens. While he was able to identify their surface proteins and genetic code, their path to reproduction—the most integral and desired information—remained elusive. His and all other attempts to revive these dead diseases have failed thus far, but that is not to say that future attempts will result in the same disappointing outcome.

Some pathogens may be more amenable to this process than others. The bacteria Bacillus anthracis, which causes the infection anthrax, for example, is known to burrow underground for long periods of time, only to rear its head at moments scientists cannot predict, sometimes taking out entire herds of animals. Since this pathogen has acquired evolutionary coping mechanisms that allow it to exist in this state of stasis, anthrax may actually be more easily manipulated when frozen.

Such an endeavor resembles the plot of a science fiction film grappling with the end of humanity as we know it, and it may seem odd to celebrate the rebirth of a once-extinct deadly disease. But, as Peterson describes, "The point, of course, is not to create zombie pathogens. Understanding the history and makeup of dead disease can help prevent future outbreaks."

Theme:

Tone:

6. A main theme of the passage is that:

- **F.** cryogenic pathogens may one day be revived in a scientific lab.
- **G.** the moral dilemma regarding the renaissance of pathogens is a difficult one.
- **H.** contradictory opinions exist as to why pathogens should be revived.
- **J.** pathogen reproduction could only be harmful to humans.

7. The tone of the passage can best be described as:

- **A.** combative and contrarian.
- **B.** informational.
- **C.** enthusiastically optimistic.
- **D.** abrasive.

8. The passage indicates that autopsies of frozen human remains can reveal all of the following EXCEPT:

- **F.** the individual's general quality of life.
- **G.** the meal the individual most often consumed.
- **H.** pathogens responsible for the individual's death.
- **J.** the individual's age.

9. The main purpose of the third paragraph (lines 23–35) is to:

- **A.** contradict the notion that frozen pathogens will never be revived.
- **B.** summarize the main argument of the passage.
- **C.** assert that all such experiments are impossible.
- **D.** transition from a general concept to the endeavor of a specific individual.

10. The passage suggests that the most important scientific advancement regarding frozen pathogens would be:

- **F.** information regarding how their genetic codes are similar to those of plants.
- **G.** a multilayer mechanism to identify their surface proteins.
- **H.** a way to identify and replicate their reproduction processes.
- **J.** a proper way to clone them.

Chapter 3

Question Categories

Key Topics
- Type 1: Specific Detail
- Type 2: Main Idea
- Type 3: Purpose

What types of ACT Reading questions will I see?
Good news: there are only 3 main categories.

- Specific detail: questions that ask you to **read** specific lines or **find** specific information in the passage
- Main idea: questions that ask you to **summarize** a whole paragraph or passage
- Purpose: questions that ask you to **analyze** why an author includes specific sentences/paragraphs

In this chapter, you'll learn how to identify each question category and then apply the appropriate strategy. The first step is to read through the passage on the following page. Annotate as you go. Promise it'll be worth it!

Not sure what annotating is? Look back at Chapter 2!

Passage I

LITERARY NARRATIVE: This passage is adapted from the novel *Elusive Origins of Me* by Toni Schmidt. (©2012 by Literacy Incorporated).

My focus fading in and out during a tenth grade psychology class, I encountered the first academic debate to which I took offense: nature vs. nurture. Apparently, centuries of philosophers and scientists had theorized and tested to see if our unique genetic codes make us who we are, or if our environments are to blame. Sure, I had black hair because I had genetically inherited that trait from my parents, but was I anxious because some chromosome had made me that way? Or did I learn that behavior watching my father pace the halls of our house during business calls? At the time, the answer seemed obvious to me: neither.

My confidence that I was unique stemmed from one fact: I had always loved music. Mother teased that I came out of the womb singing, and videos of my toddler self babbling a melody before I could even speak nearly prove that myth true. Morning, noon, and night, I devoured any record I could get a hold of. At my own home, my first taste of listening to music consisted of ten hour loops of something called "Back to Bach: Classical Guitar"—an album that my musically inept parents acquired as a gag during a White Elephant gift exchange. They slowly accumulated a larger library of listening options just for me, and after half a decade of my begging, they gave me my own guitar.

But here's the thing—neither of my parents could hum a tune. Neither could differentiate Debussy from Beethoven, nor could they properly clap to the beat of a single pop song. As far as anybody could tell, there was no way that my musical talents had been a product of my family's nurturing.

Nature was also out of the question. My mother was a scientist, born to a long lineage of scientists and mathematicians who, as my grandmother described, "never did have a taste for music." In fact, it was my mother's familially inherited love for logic puzzles that sparked her first conversation with my father on an airplane. After hearing that story throughout my childhood, I was sure that my statistician father came from similarly left-brained stock.

We couldn't be sure, however, because his parents had sent him to the United States as an infant to escape the political persecution to which they had fallen victim. The man who brought my father to the U.S. and raised him only knew the first names of my father's biological parents. The man said they hoped to join him someday but hadn't ever made it.

Although my father, stoic as ever, would never admit to desiring anything more than our little family, it was clear that he wanted to know his heritage. Once my mother and I caught onto this, we made it our mission to solve the mystery.

With the help of a professional genealogist, countless hours of research, and dozens of calls to hospitals, doctors, distant cousins, and town clerks, we did it. We traced his lineage back four generations, and I was perhaps even more shocked than he: my grandfather had been a composer. His father before him? A conductor and masterful violinist. On and on and on, a century past, musicians filled the branches of his family tree. While a classical guitar player had seemed out of place in my immediate family, my ancestors had perhaps once played, conducted, or even composed the pieces I might someday play. Generations of relatives unknown to one another were intertwined by groupings of notes on a page and how those notes could be brought alive through instrumentation.

When we presented this gift to my father, he froze—it was as if you could see the realization sweeping over him. At that moment, we understood that we were more connected than either of us had ever imagined.

Now, I can't say I've cracked the "Nature vs. Nurture" debate. While I'd still like to think that I am a musical savant, born with a stroke of inexplicable melodic genius, my journey to the genetic "nature" aspect of the argument also brought me closer to the behavioral "nurture" aspect: Although my parents had interests different from my own, they always encouraged me to follow my heart. At the whim of a toddler, they filled a house of computers and calculators with instruments and records.

Keep this passage in mind as you dive into the types of ACT Reading questions.

3.1 Type 1: Specific Detail

Specific Detail questions are the most common type of ACT Reading question, and they all work the same way. So if you can master some basic strategies, you'll be well on your way to an excellent score. Specific Detail questions will always ask you to examine specific sentences, paragraphs, or words in a passage to find an answer. A question might tell you exactly where to look (by giving a line number or a paragraph number), or you might have to find the detail yourself.

How do I know it's a Specific Detail question?
If a question requires you to find or paraphrase a detail in the passage, it's a Specific Detail question. Another way to think about it: if the question does not ask about the "main idea" or the author's "purpose," you can safely bet it's asking about a Specific Detail.

Here are some examples:

4. According to the passage, the narrator's favorite childhood album, "Back to Bach: Classical Guitar", was given to:

F. the narrator by her parents as a birthday gift.
G. the narrator's parents as a joke in a White Elephant gift exchange.
H. the narrator's father because of his love of music.
J. the narrator's mother to help her appreciate classical music more.

5. In line 56, the narrator most likely expresses shock because:

A. her ancestors had displayed talents connected to her own interests.
B. her father was unsurprised by his own heritage.
C. her father was interested in logic puzzles, which finally helped to explain her own interest in music.
D. her grandparents had pursued careers that partially explained her father's personality.

6. As it is used in line 39, the word *stock* most nearly means:

F. excess.
G. background.
H. reputation.
J. favor.

How do I answer a Specific Detail question?
The ACT uses Specific Detail questions to test one key skill: close reading. That means all you have to do is FIND the detail, and then closely read the sentences surrounding it. This might sound obvious, but the ACT is testing your ability to read precisely. The most important thing to keep in mind on Specific Detail questions is to avoid assumption and broad generalization. The ACT wants to see if you can repeat or paraphrase EXACTLY what is written.

To help you sharpen your focus and read precisely, you can tackle Specific Detail questions in 4 quick steps:

- **Step 1:** Read the question. Circle the line number or the detail you need to find. **DO NOT** read the answer choices at this point.

1. According to the passage, the narrator's favorite childhood album, "Back to Bach: Classical Guitar", was given to:

   A. the narrator by her parents as a birthday gift.
   B. the narrator's parents as a joke in a White Elephant gift exchange.
   C. the narrator's father because of his love of music.
   D. the narrator's mother to help her appreciate classical music more.

- **Step 2:** Find the detail in the text.

  Always read a few lines before and a few lines after the line reference or the detail you find. Even if the ACT says to read lines 11-14, you should start reading at line 8 or 9 and continue past line 14. If the paragraph containing the detail is small, you should simply read the whole paragraph. Why? **The answers usually appear a few lines before or after the actual lines you were given by the ACT** (or the detail you found on your own). Reading extra lines may sound time-consuming, but it will pay off.

> "Morning, noon, and night, I devoured any record I could get a hold of. At my own home, my first taste of listening to music consisted of ten hour loops of something called "Back to Bach: Classical Guitar"—an album that my musically inept parents acquired as a gag during a White Elephant gift exchange. They slowly accumulated a larger library of listening options just for me, and after half a decade of my begging, they gave me my own guitar."

- **Step 3:** ANTICIPATE the answer. Take a second to summarize what you've just read. It is important to answer the question in your own words BEFORE you look at the multiple choice answers.

  In this example, you might anticipate something like, "The parents got "Back to Bach: Classical Guitar" at a White Elephant gift exchange, but they kind of thought it was a joke."

  Don't Forget: Sometimes you'll see questions where the answers would be impossible to anticipate (like if the ACT asks you to find "Which of the following happens first?") In those cases, you can look at the answers to help guide your reading of the passage. But for the majority of questions, you can and should anticipate the answer before looking at the provided answers.

- **Step 4:** Read through the answer choices. Choose the answer that most closely matches your own.

1. According to the passage, the narrator's favorite childhood album, "Back to Bach: Classical Guitar", was given to:

   A. the narrator by her parents as a birthday gift.
   B. the narrator's parents as a joke in a White Elephant gift exchange.
   C. the narrator's father because of his love of music.
   D. the narrator's mother to help her appreciate classical music more.

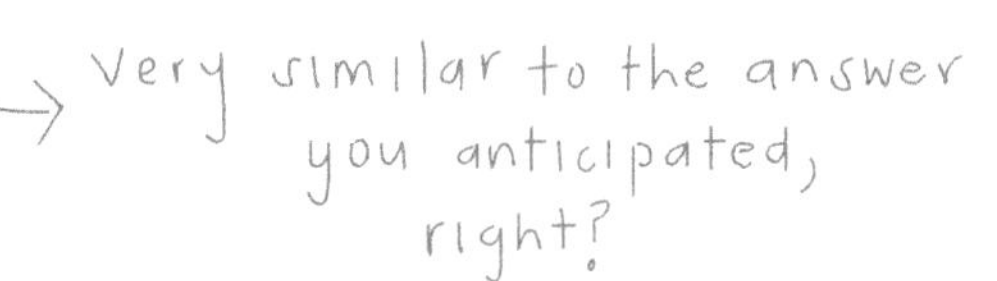

Very similar to the answer
you anticipated,
right?

But won't this take a long time?
As you practice, you'll want to gradually improve your speed at answering Specific Detail questions. Here are some tips for finding answers more quickly:

Locators
Look for **locator words** in the question: some questions contain words that are easy to find. Proper Nouns, numbers, and *italics* all stick out and should be easy to spot in long passages. Use these words to your advantage.

1. According to the passage, Coach Mark says that Cindy should:
2. Which of the following most accurately characterizes the relationship between the North American roof sparrow and homeowners?
3. Which of the following goals does the narrator state that he hopes to achieve by the age of 65?

Game Changer! **To find Locators more quickly, scan the text from end to beginning, using your finger or pencil to point at the center of the text as you go.**

By skimming backwards, you avoid accidentally re-reading the passage... which is not your goal!

Visual Mapping
Trust your spatial memory: your brain remembers where you saw certain details on the page. When you think to yourself, "I think they mentioned that at the top of the second column" or "I remember something about that toward the bottom right of the passage," you're tapping into one of your strongest natural abilities – visual memory.

If you used textual mapping (see p. 25) to annotate the passage, you can also use those notes to help locate information.

Topic Sentences
If you can't remember where to find the information in the text and the locators aren't jumping out at you, read the topic sentences of each paragraph. As you do, ask yourself, "does it sound like that information could be in this paragraph?"

So ACT Reading is just a word search?
Sometimes!

Some Specific Detail questions use phrases like "**according to the passage**," "**the passage indicates**," "**the author states**," etc. These questions are important special cases: their answers will ALWAYS be extremely literal, with minimal interpretation involved. The answer will either be an exact copy/paste or a close paraphrase of what is written in the passage:

1. The passage indicates that the narrator's father came to the U.S. because:
   A. his parents found jobs that could give the family a better life.
   B. he had decided to marry the narrator's mother.
   C. his parents had passed away, so he had been adopted by an American family.
   D. his family was experiencing political persecution.

The passage directly states the following:

> "We couldn't be sure, however, because his parents had sent him to the United States as an infant to escape the political persecution to which they had fallen victim."

Because the question uses the verb "indicates," the copy-paste language in answer choice D makes it an attractive (and correct) answer choice.

When is it more than just a word search?
So glad you asked!

Questions with words like "**most likely**," "**most nearly**," "**most reasonably be considered**", and "**implies**," or those containing **line numbers,** will require a small amount of interpretation. In these cases, answers that use copy-paste language from the text are often a trap!

1. It can most reasonably be inferred that the narrator's original assumption that she did not inherit her love for music from her father is based on:
   A. her father's career and a past interaction.
   B. a quote from her grandmother.
   C. her father's long lineage of scientists and mathematicians.
   D. her father's love for logic puzzles.

The passage directly states the following:

> "Nature was also out of the question. My mother was a scientist, born to a long lineage of scientists and mathematicians who, as my grandmother described, "never did have a taste for music." In fact, it was my mother's familially inherited love for logic puzzles that sparked her first conversation with my father on an airplane. After hearing that story throughout my childhood, I was sure that my statistician father came from similarly left-brained stock."

Because the question uses the verb "inferred," the copy-paste language of "logic puzzles" in answer choice D is likely a trap. Instead, look for answers that paraphrase the two facts you found in this paragraph: the father's job is a "statistician" and the narrator assumes he "came from similarly left-brained stock" as the narrator's mother, who was "born to a long lineage of scientists and mathematicians." Answer choice A paraphrases these details as "a past interaction" (when the father met the mother) and "his career."

Don't Forget: Even though the question contains the word "inferred," the answer isn't really an inference. "Inference" is ACT language for "paraphrase." Outside of ACT Reading, "infer" means "read between the lines." However, on the ACT, no question requires that level of critical analysis. At most, when the ACT asks you to "infer," it is simply asking you to rephrase or summarize specific details you find in the passage. Bottom line? You're always looking for the answer choice that sticks closest to the meaning of the original text, with no assumption or true inference allowed.

Now, you try. Use the passage on p. 46 to answer these Specific Detail questions.

1. In line 56, the narrator most likely expresses shock because:

A. her ancestors had displayed talents connected to her own interests.
B. her father was unsurprised by his own heritage.
C. her father was interested in logic puzzles, which finally helped to explain her own interest in music.
D. her grandparents had pursued careers that partially explained her father's personality.

2. As it is used in line 39, the word *stock* most nearly means:

F. excess.
G. background.
H. reputation.
J. favor.

3. In line 67, the phrase "this gift" most nearly refers to:

A. an instrument given to the narrator's father.
B. the narrator's new maturity and perspective.
C. the revealed identities of the narrator's father's ancestors.
D. a compelling question about the narrator's father's parents.

4. It can most reasonably be inferred that Beethoven is an example of a musician whom:

F. the narrator and her parents both admire.
G. the narrator's parents do not like.
H. the narrator knows well, though her parents do not.
J. the narrator finds it difficult to distinguish from Debussy.

5. According to the passage, the narrator's mother is a scientist, and her father is:

A. also a scientist.
B. a musician.
C. a business owner.
D. a statistician.

Answer Key:

1. A
   - Find the specific detail in the text: "We traced his lineage back four generations, and I was perhaps even more shocked than he: my grandfather had been a composer. His father before him? A conductor and masterful violinist. On and on and on, a century past, musicians filled the branches of his family tree. While a classical guitar player had seemed out of place in my immediate family, my ancestors had perhaps once played, conducted, or even composed the pieces I might someday play."
   - Anticipate: The narrator was shocked because her ancestors were musically inclined, just like the narrator.
   - Answer: Answer choice A matches best, describing their musical natures as "talents connected to her own interests."
2. G
   - Find the specific detail in the text: "In fact, it was my mother's familially inherited love for logic puzzles that sparked her first conversation with my father on an airplane. After hearing that story throughout my childhood, I was sure that my statistician father came from similarly left-brained stock."
   - Anticipate: "...I was sure that my statistician father came from similar family traits."
   - Answer: Answer choice G is closest to the anticipated answer, and is therefore correct!
3. C
   - Find the specific detail in the text: The sentence that contains the lines is at the beginning of a new paragraph, so you should start reading in the previous paragraph. In lines 54–57, you will find the sentence, "We traced his lineage back four generations, and I was perhaps even more shocked than he: my grandfather had been a composer."
   - Anticipate: The narrator found her father's ancestors.
   - Answer: Answer choice C closely paraphrases the sentences found in the passage.
4. H
   - Find the specific detail in the text: Since the question does not provide a line number, use the name Beethoven as a locator. In lines 27–29, the sentence mentions Beethoven: "Neither could differentiate Debussy from Beethoven, nor could they properly clap to the beat of a single pop song."
   - Anticipate: The parents are not familiar with Beethoven.
   - Answer: This leads us to the answer choice H, which paraphrases the sentences found in the passage.
5. D
   - Find the specific detail in the text: The best locators here are to find where the narrator talks about "mother" and "scientist". These keywords are found in the fourth paragraph. Keep reading, and you will find the phrase "my statistician father."
   - Anticipate: Statistician! Notice that the question says "According to the passage," making a copy-paste anticipation totally acceptable.
   - Answer: D, of course!

3.2 Type 2: Main Idea

These questions ask you to **summarize** paragraphs or entire passages. The goal will be to look for main arguments: What is the central point the paragraph is trying to get at? What is the overall argument of the passage?

How do I identify a Main Idea question?
These ones are pretty easy to spot. The question might literally ask you about the "main idea" of a paragraph or passage. Other times, the question will use key phrases like, "the passage draws which of the following conclusions," or "the passage can best be described as," which tell you, yes, this is a "main idea" question.

Here are some examples:

1. The main idea of the third paragraph (lines 26–31) can best be summarized as:

- **A.** the narrator's parents are interested primarily in logic and math.
- **B.** the interests of the narrator's parents explain the narrator's own personality.
- **C.** the narrator's love of music can be connected to her parents' love of Bach.
- **D.** the narrator's parents do not share her love of music.

2. The narrator draws which of the following conclusions after considering the question of nature vs. nurture?

- **F.** Nature is stronger than nurture, as is illustrated by the long line of musicians in the father's family.
- **G.** Nature and nurture both play some role in shaping identity.
- **H.** Nurture does not contribute to identity because the narrator's parents discouraged her from becoming a musician.
- **J.** Nurture determines identity.

How do I answer a Main Idea question?
Here's a simple formula: Theme + Tone = Main Idea.

To find the theme and tone, use these helpful strategies:

First, Read the Conclusion
If you are asked to find the main idea of the entire passage, go straight to the conclusion paragraph. On the ACT Reading section, conclusions are even more important than introductions. Conclusions are where authors re-assert, summarize, wrap up, put a bow on, bring home—you get the idea—their main points.

> To answer #2 above, look in the example passage. The conclusion begins with the sentence, "Now, I can't say I've cracked the "Nature vs. Nurture" debate," implying the author hasn't reached a solid conclusion.

Next, Read the Title
Sounds simple, but it works. If you are summarizing the entire passage, titles often give important clues to the author's main idea. Sometimes they'll even give away the main argument.

> This passage is adapted from a work titled *Elusive Origins of Me.* Again, this suggests that a main theme of the passage is the narrator's confusion about where aspects of her identity come from.

Tone

Most of the time, the correct answers to Main Idea questions will match the author's tone. You can eliminate answer choices that do not match the tone at all—for example, if an answer choice contains words that give it a negative tone, but you know the tone of the passage is positive, the answer is most likely incorrect.

> Look through the emotional language of the passage. Words like "anxious" (line 8) and "shocked" (line 56) suggest the tone of the passage might best be described as questioning. This is neither entirely positive nor negative, which is still very useful: it will be smart to eliminate answers that contain absolutely positive or negative language.

Putting it all Together

When you put together what you learn from the conclusion, the title, and the tone of the passage, you can see an emphasis on the narrator's confusion and indecisiveness.

The passage suggests both nurture *and* nature play a role in shaping identity.

Look back at the multiple choice answers. Answer choice **G** is the only choice that includes both nature *and* nurture.

Don't Forget: When Main Idea questions ask you to find the main idea of a single paragraph, make sure you are summarizing **only** the given paragraph, not the passage as a whole. Read the full paragraph, but pay careful attention to the **first** and **last** sentences, rather than the conclusion and title. **Tone** is also still valuable.

Try it!

1. One main idea of the passage is that:

A. parents should encourage their children to focus on career-oriented skills.
B. a study of genealogy is required for people who do not know their lineage.
C. studying music is a necessary part of a child's upbringing.
D. the narrator is influenced by both her family history and childhood upbringing.

2. The main idea of the first paragraph is that:

F. the narrator disagrees with the concept of nature vs. nurture.
G. genetics determine how a person will look and behave.
H. behavior is learned from one's childhood environment.
J. the narrator enjoys enthusiastically debating nature vs. nurture.

3. The narrator's tone in the seventh paragraph (lines 52–66) can best be described as:

A. defiant and critical.
B. surprised and excited.
C. casual and flippant.
D. whimsical yet cold.

Answer Key

1. D

 - Main Idea of the entire passage. Go straight to the conclusion paragraph: The narrator sees truth in both aspects of the nature vs. nurture debate and gives examples for each. She mentions being "born with a stroke of inexplicable melodic genius," but says that her parents "always encouraged me to follow my heart."
 - Read the Title: "Elusive Origins of Me" indicates that the narrator's origins are unclear.
 - Answer D includes *both* "family history" (nature) and "childhood."

2. F

 - Main Idea of one paragraph. Read the intro sentence: The narrator says that she "takes offense" to the debate of nature vs. nurture, so she likely doesn't agree with one or the other completely.
 - Read the paragraph's concluding sentence: The narrator feels that neither nature nor nurture completely determine a person's traits.
 - Note the Tone: Words like "offense" (line 3) and the sarcastic use of "apparently" (line 3) signal the narrator's disagreement.
 - Answer F matches the tone ("disagrees") and the topic ("the distinction between nature and nurture").

3. B

 - Note the Tone: Words like "shocked" (line 56) indicate that this revelation was unexpected. In lines 69–70, ("...we understood that we were more connected than either of us had ever imagined"), we see that this is positive news for the narrator and her father.
 - Eliminate: We are looking for a positive tone that indicates surprise. "Defiant and critical" and "cold" are both negative. "Casual and flippant" are neutral. Answer B matches the tone.

3.3 Type 3: Purpose

These questions are different from all other ACT Reading questions for one important reason: they do not ask you to find or summarize what is written in the passage. Instead, they ask you *why* a particular sentence, phrase, paragraph, or passage was written in the first place. Why is a particular phrase effective? What is the function of a paragraph?

How do I identify a Purpose question?
Like all ACT Reading question types, Purpose questions often include the same key phrases over and over again. Phrases like "the purpose," "primary function", "serves to", and "in order to" all suggest you are reading a Purpose question.

Here's an example:

1. The primary purpose of the seventh paragraph (lines 52–66) is to:

A. continue to reinforce the narrator's descriptions of her family's long history of musical expertise.
B. introduce unexpected information that shifts the narrator's thinking.
C. show an unanticipated relationship to the professional genealogist.
D. demonstrate the narrator's incessant obsession with determining if traits come from nature or nurture.

How do I answer a Purpose question?
Think like the author. If you keep in mind that every passage is written by a person with an agenda, you'll realize that every sentence, every word, every paragraph is a choice. Someone put it there for a reason. Your job is to figure out that reason. The following steps will get you there:

- **Step 1:** Identify if the question asks about the purpose of a Specific Detail or the purpose of a Main Idea.
  - If the Purpose question asks about a specific paragraph or a specific detail, start the same way you would for any Specific Detail question: find the paragraph, or the detail, in the passage.
  - If the purpose question asks about the entire passage, start the same way you would for any Main Idea question: read the conclusion and the title, and identify the tone of the passage.
- **Step 2:** Paraphrase what you've read.
  - Just as you did with the Anticipate step of Specific Detail questions, make sure you can paraphrase the information in your own words.
- **Step 3:** This is the important one. Purpose questions are NOT about summarizing what's written. Instead, ask yourself, "Why would someone write this?"
  - Because they want to change the subject? Refute a point? Provide a specific example to support a general point? Use an expert opinion to back up an earlier point?
  - If you're having trouble anticipating the purpose on your own, use the answer choices. Read each and ask yourself, "Does the purpose (Step 3) apply to the paraphrase (Step 2)?"

1. The primary purpose of the seventh paragraph (lines 52–66) is to:

A. continue to reinforce the narrator's descriptions of her family's long history of musical expertise.
B. introduce unexpected information that shifts the narrator's thinking.
C. show an unanticipated relationship to the professional genealogist.
D. demonstrate the narrator's incessant obsession with determining if traits come from nature or nurture.

- **Step 1:** This question is about a specific paragraph, so read through the seventh paragraph.
- **Step 2:** Your paraphrase might sound something like: "The narrator's family does in fact have a history of musical excellence, which is a shock to both the narrator and her father."
- **Step 3:** Earlier paragraphs suggested that neither the narrator nor her parents seemed to have any musical skill or predisposition. Therefore, this paragraph represents a turning point. It is the first time the narrator acknowledges that genetics may play some role in shaping her musical talent.

Looking through the answer choices, **B** most closely mirrors the answer to Step 3. That is the correct answer!

Any other advice for answering purpose questions?
Not surprisingly, yes!

Use the Verbs!
When choosing an answer to Purpose questions, look for verbs in the answer choices. For example, an answer might say the author uses a sentence to "continue," "shift," "illustrate," "demonstrate," or "provide an example." If a verb is inaccurate, you can eliminate the entire answer. And if a verb seems correct, that's a clue that the whole answer might be correct. In the example above, the verbs are "continue," "shift," "show," and "demonstrate." Because this paragraph functions as an important turning point in which the author finds proof to support their argument, "shift" is a tempting answer choice. "Shift" is the verb that highlights the contrast inherent in this paragraph.

Identify the Perspective and Point of View
Because Purpose questions require you to think like the author, it is important to identify the perspective and the point-of-view of the author. The perspective refers to the position of the author in relation to their subject: for example, is the author a child or an adult looking back on childhood? Is the author writing in the present, past, or future tense? The point-of-view refers to first-person, second-person, or third-person narration. More on those terms on the next page!

rhetoric is language that is used in order to have a specific effect on an audience

Know your rhetorical terms!

Answers to purpose questions often include the following rhetorical terms. You'll need to know them to answer purpose questions confidently!

Rhetorical Term	Definition	Example
Assertion	A confident claim. Assertions are often followed by supporting evidence or explanation.	"Standardized tests should be illegal." "It is unlikely that scientists will ever discover life beyond the solar system, even if that life exists."
Flashback	An event that happened before the current time in which the main story is set.	"All the children gathered around their grandmother; no one told better stories. She cleared her throat loudly and began as she always did: "When I was a little girl, times were different than they are today. . . "
Irony	The opposite of what is expected or anticipated, often in a comical sense.	"Our pool was swept away by the rising waters of the river." "As I waited for my doctor to see me (my sinus infection was getting worse), I caught a terrible cold from the man coughing next to me."
Limited Point of View	Only one character's thoughts and feelings are known.	"Jayne loved the smell of fresh roses nearly as much as she loved watching her mother make the bouquets."
Omniscient Point of View	All characters' thoughts and feelings are known.	"Jayne loved the smell of fresh roses. Her mother secretly loved lilies, but, year after year, she found herself indulging her daughter's preferences."
First-Person Point of View	The narrator is telling his or her own story.	"I always loved the springtime because Mama made sure fresh flowers were in a vase on every tabletop in our home."
Third-person point of view	The narrator is telling someone else's story.	"Jayne always loved the springtime because her mother made sure fresh flowers were in a vase on every tabletop in their house."
Rhetorical question	A question asked in order to make a point, rather than to get an answer.	"Are political opponents still capable of constructive, open-minded debate?"
Figurative language	Any language that is not meant literally. Figurative language includes simile and metaphor. It also includes the personification of non-living things.	"My brother is a mole, never leaving his room except to eat." "The wind grabbed her by the coat and threw her to the ground."
Anecdote	A short story of an interesting or amusing personal incident.	"I remember the first time my mother took our new dog, Fredo, for a walk. He pulled her ceaselessly down the street, finally dragging her into Mr. Edison's prized vegetable garden."
Idiomatic Expressions	Informal expressions commonly understood to mean more than what the words literally state.	"She was furious at the injustice of the grading system. But when she confronted the professor, she knew enough to hold her tongue."
Sensory Detail	A detail that refers to one of the five senses: sight, smell, taste, touch, hearing.	"The ripe peach's sweet scent filled the air as I bit into it, the rich juices dripping down my cheeks."

Try it! Use the passage on p. 46.

1. The author most likely includes the question "Or did I learn that behavior watching my father pace the halls during business calls?" (lines 9–11) in order to:

   A. articulate one side of the passage's central debate.
   B. illustrate the absurdity of the theory that nurture determines personality.
   C. explain why the narrator finds it difficult to sit still.
   D. provide an example of the father's anxious personality.

2. The primary function of lines 14–17 is to:

   F. relate an anecdote from the narrator's childhood.
   G. contrast the statement made in the previous sentence.
   H. summarize the narrator's feelings about her mother.
   J. list the narrator's favorite songs from when she was a child.

3. The point of view from which the passage is written is best described as:

   A. first-person limited.
   B. first-person omniscient.
   C. third-person limited.
   D. third-person omniscient.

Answer Key:

1. A

    - Your job is to consider WHY this question is included, NOT to give a summary of the phrase at hand. Even though the sentence does "provide an example of the father's anxious personality," that doesn't explain WHY the author included this sentence.
    - If you read the remainder of the paragraph, you see that the author is introducing their argument regarding nature vs. nurture. The sentence prior explains that while physical traits (like "black hair") are inherited genetically (nature), the author wonders if personality traits are as well. The sentence you are analyzing functions as a continuation of that musing—rather than inheriting anxiety through chromosomes, was it the narrator's observations of the father that caused an anxious personality to develop?
    - The concluding sentence (the author determines that neither was solely responsible) again reinforces this idea that the purpose of this sentence is to (A) articulate (or explain) one side of the passage's central argument (nurture can be responsible for a person's traits).

2. F

    - Why did the author include these lines? Here, the narrator simply relates a brief story that illustrates how passionately she has always loved music, seemingly from the day she was born. The purpose of these lines is to provide a story that the author uses as an example to further their argument.

3. A

    - This passage uses the words "I" and "my," so you know that the passage is in the first-person. While you know the author's thoughts and feelings, you don't know anyone else's. That means the point of view is limited.

3.4 Chapter Test

You've completed Chapter 3! Just to recap, you should now have a general understanding of the three types of questions and how to answer them:

- Specific Detail
- Main Idea
- Purpose

The Chapter Test on the following pages will test these skills. Use it as an opportunity to try out everything you've learned from this chapter as best you can. That requires coordinating a lot of moving pieces, so be patient with yourself and just do your best!

CHAPTER TEST

DIRECTIONS: Read the passages and answer the questions that follow. Use the blanks provided to categorize each question as (S) Specific Detail, (M) Main Idea, or (P) Purpose and use the appropriate steps. The following passages have been shortened; the point here is to practice your Critical Reading skills. Don't worry about timing yet—you'll learn how to manage the clock in Chapter 4.

Passage II

SOCIAL SCIENCE: This passage is adapted from the article "Balancing Economic Bliss" by Gomer Alvarado (©2018 by Happiness Associate Print).

"Money can't buy you happiness." A comfort in times of need, a corrective in times of excess, this saying has been embraced through centuries of human economic endeavors. The possession of material goods, it 5 claims, cannot by itself create happiness; instead, individuals can achieve emotional well-being only by searching for meaning beyond the almighty dollar, in interpersonal relationships and meaningful experiences. It's an important philosophical claim about the human condition. Psy- 10 chologically speaking, however, no simple adage can capture the nuanced relationship between contentment and wealth.

Historically, academics have bought into the "money can't buy you happiness" psychological model, 15 but with one important caveat: an individual or population must first attain a certain threshold of economic security. A landmark psychological study conducted at Barnett University in 1973 showed that adults within developed nations who made enough money to take care 20 of their basic needs tended to be happier than those who didn't. Reasonable enough, but the researchers also came to this startling conclusion: individuals who achieved wealth significantly above the "basic needs" threshold were no happier than those barely above it. Essentially, 25 distance from the threshold was irrelevant; the only thing that mattered was whether one was above or below. A new study from Smithson University seems to corroborate and expand upon the findings: although living standards and consumer spending are on the rise globally, ma- 30 terial prosperity above the basic needs threshold has not correlated with higher levels of happiness.

So when it comes to happiness, why do we consistently find such diminishing returns on income? Some insight might come from the observed contrast between the 35 happiness of city versus country dwellers. By most measures, without money, life in the city is worse. Individuals who live in urban areas incur higher costs of living than those in rural areas, making rigorous work schedules more a necessity than a choice. Simultaneously, these in- 40 dividuals forfeit opportunities for free happiness that correlate with the great outdoors. Because they cannot enjoy fresh air and outdoor activity to the same extent as non-city-dwellers, they pour expendable income into technology and material goods that make city life more enjoy- 45 able. Gadgets and clothes become approximate substitutes for nature and free social gatherings in the homes of friends. The result is a classic cycle: city dwellers must work to obtain the material goods that make their lives more enjoyable, the material goods deplete income, and 50 the work must continue. The cycle blocks city-dwellers from ever finding the free goods that might otherwise foster happiness.

What does this mean for individuals hoping (and who isn't?) to maximize happiness? Studies suggest that 55 location plays some significant role when it comes to assessing both the possible degrees of joy and the means of obtaining happiness. For those living in rural areas, happiness is more free than many realize. For those living in cities, which restrict access to free happiness, it seems 60 that money might help, in some crude way, compensate for what has been lost.

1. _____ One main idea of the passage is that:

   A. physical locale is the greatest predictor of happiness.
   B. relative income is the greatest predictor of happiness.
   C. happiness can be measured by multiple metrics.
   D. human sources of happiness remain elusive to researchers.

2. _____ In the context of the passage, the author's use of the phrase "Money...happiness" (line 1) most likely serves to:

   F. create a lighthearted and familiar introduction to the topic of the passage.
   G. state a claim that the author will later completely contradict.
   H. formulate the hypothesis on which this passage is based.
   J. offer expert evidence on a claim stated later in the passage.

3. _____ As it is used in line 17, the word *landmark* most nearly means:

   A. physical location.
   B. breakthrough.
   C. achievement.
   D. unimportant.

4. _____ The primary function of the third paragraph (lines 32–52) is to:

   F. transition from the conclusions of a study to conclusions drawn from observation.
   G. compare various aforementioned studies.
   H. assert an untestable claim.
   J. admit the limitations of the study from Smithson University.

5. _____ Which of the following best paraphrases the author's comments in lines 47–50?

   A. The cycle from poverty to wealth creates free opportunities for happiness that may have been previously overlooked.
   B. Individuals who live in cities are, on average, less happy than those who live in rural areas.
   C. On average, urban populations work more to create happiness and therefore forgo free goods that might likewise create happiness.
   D. Cost of living now makes it impossible for people to take advantage of the free goods they once enjoyed.

6. _____ According to the passage, the study conducted at Smithson University:

   F. added a new metric for researchers to consider.
   G. agreed with previously accepted conclusions within a modern context.
   H. created a cycle of consuming.
   J. became the only valid study within a subset of psychology.

7. _____ Which of the following is true of the study conducted at Barnett University?

   A. The study was valid only in regards to developed nations.
   B. Economic wealth had little to no influence on happiness.
   C. The results suggested that there was little correlation between money and worry.
   D. Individuals with lesser living standards led happier lives.

8. _____ The main idea of the last paragraph is that:

   F. the results of this particular study indicate that happiness has no specific origin.
   G. location can play a role in how people can find happiness.
   H. further research may prove research about locale to be false.
   J. happiness should be the primary consideration when it comes to choosing where to live.

9. _____ The author's tone can generally be described as:

   A. informative and insightful.
   B. humorous yet sympathetic.
   C. appreciative and sarcastic.
   D. optimistic yet cautious.

10. _____ It can most reasonably be inferred from the passage that the author includes the statement in lines 45–47 ("Gadgets and clothes...of friends") in order to:

    F. define a term.
    G. further a previous claim with a more concrete example.
    H. expand upon the previous idea with a new one.
    J. contrast the idea that precedes it.

Passage III

HUMANITIES: This passage is adapted from the book *The Angelou* by Kristine Britton (©2018 by Childsplay Press).

Maya Angelou is one of the most acclaimed American authors of the twentieth century. Known for her poetry, autobiographies, and essays, as well as her civil rights activism, Angelou lived to the age of 86. Throughout her long life, she created works that found a key place in American culture, and during her lifetime, she was the recipient of more than 50 honorary degrees. She left the world with a catalog of extraordinary writing.

But Angelou didn't start her life as Maya Angelou at all. Marguerite Annie Johnson was born in St. Louis in 1928. As a child, she kept a journal and wrote essays and poetry, demonstrating an interest in books, literature, and writing from a young age. After spending her childhood with various family members, Angelou moved to California with her brother and mother at age 14. She earned a scholarship to study dance and drama at the California Labor School, but she left at age 16. She took a job as a cable car conductor in San Francisco, becoming the first Black woman to hold the position. Normally a job reserved for men, the role was opened to women during World War II as men left to join the service. Although she was at first told not to apply because of her race, Angelou returned to the office daily for three weeks until the company acquiesced.

Upon leaving the cable car conductor job, Angelou returned to high school. A few weeks after graduating, she gave birth to a son. In addition to working as a waitress and cook to support herself and her child, Angelou continued to write. But writing was not Angelou's only creative pursuit. As a young mother in the 1950s, she took on a gig as a nightclub singer. Her career as a performer took her to Europe to tour with the opera Porgy and Bess, and she studied modern dance with the renowned Martha Graham and performed with Alvin Ailey. She took on the name Maya Angelou as a stage name of sorts, Maya coming from her childhood nickname and Angelou from Angelos, her former married surname.

At the end of the decade, she joined the Harlem Writers Guild. The group was founded in the 1940s by Black writers who were excluded from the literary culture of New York. With the support of another famous writer, James Baldwin, Angelou began work on her first novel, *I Know Why the Caged Bird Sings*. For years, her debut novel was banned in many schools because of her frank writing about the abuse she suffered as a child. Despite the attempted censorship, the book provided a model of strength through enduring trauma and a voice that resonated with readers with similar experiences who were grateful to an author who wasn't afraid to speak to subjects that were often considered taboo.

Angelou's experiences with childhood abuse were a foundational part of her story. The man who abused her was convicted, but only jailed for one day; four days after his release, he was killed. At the age of 8, Angelou became mute for nearly five years: she felt like her voice was so powerful that it could kill. It seems like no coincidence that when Angelou began to speak again, she became one of the most powerful voices in poetry and in activism.

Activism in the civil rights movement was core to Angelou's life. Her relationship with South African freedom fighter Vusumzi Make took her to Cairo, and she later moved to Accra, Ghana. There, she met Malcolm X; in 1965, she returned to the United States to help create a new civil rights organization. She witnessed the LA riots in 1965 and continued the fight when she agreed to organize a march for Dr. Martin Luther King Jr. in 1968. These events led her to create a documentary series about the connection between Black American heritage and blues music on what is now PBS. Angelou returned to the American South in the 1980s to come to terms with her life there; she spent decades as a professor at Wake Forest University in Winston-Salem, North Carolina.

In 2011, President Barack Obama presented Angelou with the Presidential Medal of Freedom as a symbol of her importance to the United States. Even in her later years, Angelou continued to write, publishing the seventh volume of her autobiography in 2013 at age 85. She died at age 86 and will be known to history as an important part of the American story.

11. _____ The main idea of the passage is that:

A. Malcolm X was a major figure in Maya Angelou's life and work.
B. writing is the most important artistic medium.
C. Maya Angelou made contributions to American culture through her writing and activism.
D. Maya Angelou's life story is an example of the American struggle.

12. _____ As it is used in line 24, the word *acquiesced* most nearly means:

F. agreed to hire her.
G. refused to hire her.
H. persisted in hiring her.
J. publicized her hire.

13. _____ It can most reasonably be inferred that the Harlem Writers Guild:

A. was founded by James Baldwin.
B. published Maya Angelou's first novel, *I Know Why the Caged Bird Sings.*
C. was a supportive group of Black writers in New York founded in the 1950s.
D. was an organization to which Maya Angelou belonged.

14. _____ Which of the following jobs did Maya Angelou NOT have?

F. Ballet dancer
G. Cook
H. Cable car conductor
J. Waitress

15. _____ Which of the following events mentioned in the passage occurred first chronologically?

A. Angelou moved to Accra, Ghana.
B. Angelou moved to North Carolina.
C. Angelou moved to California.
D. Angelou moved to Cairo.

16. _____ The main purpose of the fifth paragraph (lines 51-59) is to:

F. detail the trauma Angelou endured.
G. provide background information regarding a childhood experience that impacted Angelou's life and work.
H. summarize the plot of Angelou's first novel, I *Know Why the Caged Bird Sings.*
J. interrogate a narrative that inspired a foundational part of Angelou's work.

17. _____ According to the passage, Angelou published how many volumes of her autobiography?

A. Seven
B. Fourteen
C. Fifty
D. Eighty-six

18. _____ Which of the following questions is directly answered by the passage?

F. What accomplishment was Angelou most proud of?
G. At what university was Angelou a professor?
H. What was the name of Angelou's son?
J. What year was Angelou's first novel published?

19. _____ Based on the passage, Marguerite Annie Johnson chose to go by Maya Angelou because:

A. she wanted to honor her family with a stage name that referenced her father's name, Angelos.
B. as a touring performer, she required a stage name.
C. she wanted to honor the nickname given to her by Martha Graham and Alvin Ailey.
D. the name referenced a childhood nickname and her ex-husband's last name.

20. _____ Maya Angelou's involvement in the civil rights movement:

F. inspired her to create a new civil rights organization based in Cairo and Ghana.
G. was an integral part of her life, especially as she became older.
H. led her to work with Martin Luther King, Jr. to create a documentary series.
J. motivated her to write a celebrated novel about the connection between Black American heritage and blues music.

Answer Key

Key
S = Specific Detail
M = Main Idea
P = Purpose

1. One main idea of the passage is that:

Skim the Last Paragraph: Lines 53–61

M

What does this mean for individuals hoping (and who isn't?) to maximize happiness? Studies suggest that location plays some significant role when it comes to assessing both the possible degrees of joy and the means of obtaining happiness. For those living in rural areas, happiness is more free than many realize. For those living in cities, which restrict access to free happiness, it seems that money might help, in some crude way, compensate for what has been lost.

A. physical locale is the greatest predictor of happiness.
B. relative income is the greatest predictor of happiness.
C. happiness can be measured by multiple metrics.
D. human sources of happiness remain completely elusive to researchers.

2. In the context of the passage, the author's use of the phrase "Money...happiness" (line 1) most likely serves to:

Read in full context: Lines 1–8

"'Money can't buy you happiness." A comfort in times of need, a corrective in times of excess, this saying has been embraced through centuries of human economic endeavors. The possession of material goods, it claims, cannot by itself create happiness; instead, individuals can achieve emotional well-being only by searching for meaning beyond the almighty dollar, in interpersonal relationships and meaningful experiences.

F. create a lighthearted and familiar introduction to the topic of the passage.
G. state a claim that the author will later contradict.
H. formulate the hypothesis on which this passage is based.
J. offer expert evidence on a claim stated later in the passage.

3. As it is used in line 17, the word *landmark* most nearly means:

Read in full context: Lines 13–22

Historically, academics have bought into the "money can't buy you happiness" psychological model, but with one important caveat: an individual or population must first attain a certain threshold of economic security. A landmark psychological study conducted at Barnett University in 1973 showed that adults within developed nations who made enough money to take care of their basic needs tended to be happier than those who didn't. Reasonable enough, but the researchers also came to this startling conclusion....

A. physical location.
B. breakthrough.
C. achievement.
D. unimportant.

4. The primary function of the third paragraph (lines 32–52) is to:

Read in full context: Lines 32–35

P *So when it comes to happiness, why do we consistently find such diminishing returns on income? Some insight might come from the observed contrast between the happiness of city versus country dwellers.*

F. transition from the conclusions of a study to conclusions drawn from observation.
G. compare various aforementioned studies.
H. assert an untestable claim.
J. admit the limitations of the study from Smithson University.

5. Which of the following best paraphrases the author's comments in lines 47–50?

Read in full context: Lines 47–52

S *The result is a classic cycle: city dwellers must work to obtain the material goods that make their lives more enjoyable, the material goods deplete income, and the work must continue. The cycle blocks city-dwellers from ever finding the free goods that might otherwise foster happiness.*

A. The cycle from poverty to wealth creates free opportunities for happiness that may have been previously overlooked.
B. Individuals who live in cities are, on average, less happy than those who live in rural areas.
C. On average, urban populations work more to create happiness and therefore forgo free goods that might likewise create happiness.
D. Cost of living now makes it impossible for people to take advantage of the free goods they once enjoyed.

6. According to the passage, the study conducted at Smithson University:

Find and read in full context: Lines 26–31

S *A new study from Smithson University seems to corroborate and expand upon the findings: although living standards and consumer spending are on the rise globally, material prosperity above the basic needs threshold has not correlated with higher levels of happiness.*

F. added a new metric for researchers to consider.
G. agreed with previously accepted conclusions within a modern context.
H. created a cycle of consuming.
J. became the only valid study within a subset of psychology.

7. Which of the following is true of the study conducted at Barnett University?

Find and read in full context: Lines 13–24

Historically, academics have bought into the "money can't buy you happiness" psychological model, but with one important caveat: an individual or population must first attain a certain threshold of economic security. A landmark psychological study conducted at Barnett University in 1973 showed that adults within developed nations who made enough money to take care of their basic needs tended to be happier than those who didn't. Reasonable enough, but the researchers also came to this startling conclusion: individuals who achieved wealth significantly above the "basic needs" threshold were no happier than those barely above it.

A. The study was valid only in regards to developed nations.
B. Economic wealth had little to no influence on happiness.
C. The results suggested that there was little correlation between money and worry.
D. Individuals with lesser living standards led happier lives.

8. The main idea of the last paragraph is that:

Read in full context: Lines 53–61

What does this mean for individuals hoping (and who isn't?) to maximize happiness? Studies suggest that location plays some significant role when it comes to assessing both the possible degrees of joy and the means of obtaining happiness. For those living in rural areas, happiness is more free than many realize. For those living in cities, which restrict access to free happiness, it seems that money might help, in some crude way, compensate for what has been lost.

F. the results of this particular study indicate that happiness has no specific origin.
G. location can play a role in how people can find happiness.
H. further research may prove the apparent link between location and happiness to be false.
J. happiness should be the primary consideration when it comes to choosing where to live.

9. The author's tone can generally be described as:

Look for emotion words in the passage. For example: Lines 9–12 and 26–31

Psychologically speaking, however, no simple adage can capture the nuanced relationship between contentment and wealth.

A new study from Smithson University seems to corroborate and expand upon the findings: although living standards and consumer spending are on the rise globally, material prosperity above the basic needs threshold has not correlated with higher levels of happiness.

The wording of the passage is mostly neutral, and the author conveys results from other studies rather than their own opinion.

A. informative and insightful.
B. humorous yet sympathetic.
C. appreciative and sarcastic.
D. optimistic yet cautious.

10. It can most reasonably be inferred from the passage that the author includes the statement in lines 45–47 (Gadgets and clothes...of friends) in order to:

Read in full context: Lines 41–50

> *Because they cannot enjoy fresh air and outdoor activity to the same extent as non-city-dwellers, they pour expendable income into technology and material goods that make city life more enjoyable. Gadgets and clothes become approximate substitutes for nature and free social gatherings in the homes of friends. The result is a classic cycle: city dwellers must work to obtain the material goods that make their lives more enjoyable, the material goods deplete income, and the work must continue.*

F. define a term.
G. further a previous claim with a more concrete example.
H. expand upon the previous idea with a new one.
J. contrast the idea that precedes it.

11. The main idea of the passage is that:

Skim the last paragraph: Lines 74–80

> *In 2011, President Barack Obama presented Angelou with the Presidential Medal of Freedom as a symbol of her importance to the United States. Even in her later years, Angelou continued to write, publishing the seventh volume of her autobiography in 2013 at age 85. She died at age 86 and will be known to history as an important part of the American story.*

A. Malcolm X was a major figure in Maya Angelou's life and work.
B. writing is the most important artistic medium.
C. Maya Angelou made contributions to American culture through her writing and activism.
D. Maya Angelou's life story is an example of the American struggle.

12. As it is used in line 24, the word *acquiesced* most nearly means:

Read in full context: Lines 21–24

> *Although she was at first told not to apply because of her race, Angelou returned to the office daily for three weeks until the company acquiesced.*

F. agreed to hire her.
G. refused to hire her.
H. persisted in hiring her.
J. publicized her hire.

13. It can most reasonably be inferred that the Harlem Writers Guild:

Find and read in full context: Lines 38–41

> *At the end of the decade, she joined the Harlem Writers Guild. The group was founded in the 1940s by Black writers who were excluded from the literary culture of New York.*

A. was founded by James Baldwin.
B. published Maya Angelou's first novel, *I Know Why the Caged Bird Sings.*
C. was a supportive group of Black writers in New York founded in the 1950s.
D. was an organization to which Maya Angelou belonged.

14. Which of the following jobs did Maya Angelou NOT have?

Find and read in full context: Lines 25-34

> *Upon leaving the cable car conductor job, Angelou returned to high school. A few weeks after graduating, she gave birth to a son. In addition to working as a waitress and cook to support herself and her child, Angelou continued to write. But writing was not Angelou's only creative pursuit. As a young mother in the 1950s, she took on a gig as a nightclub singer. Her career as a performer took her to Europe to tour with the opera Porgy and Bess, and she studied modern dance with the renowned Martha Graham and performed with Alvin Ailey.*

F. Ballet dancer
G. Cook
H. Cable car conductor
J. Waitress

15. Which of the following events mentioned in the passage occurred first chronologically?

Look for time words: Lines 13–15

> *After spending her childhood with various family members, Angelou moved to California with her brother and mother at age 14.*

A. Angelou moved to Accra, Ghana.
B. Angelou moved to North Carolina.
C. Angelou moved to California.
D. Angelou moved to Cairo.

16. The main purpose of the fifth paragraph (lines 51–59) is to:

Read in full context: Lines 51–59

P

Angelou's experiences with childhood abuse were a foundational part of her story. The man who abused her was convicted, but only jailed for one day; four days after his release, he was killed. At the age of 8, Angelou became mute for nearly five years: she felt like her voice was so powerful that it could kill. It seems like no coincidence that when Angelou began to speak again, she became one of the most powerful voices in poetry and in activism.

F. detail the trauma Angelou endured.
G. provide background information regarding a childhood experience that impacted Angelou's life and work.
H. summarize the plot of Angelou's first novel, I *Know Why the Caged Bird Sings*.
J. interrogate a narrative that inspired a foundational part of Angelou's work.

17. According to the passage, Angelou published how many volumes of her autobiography?

Find and read in full context: Lines 76–78

S

Even in her later years, Angelou continued to write, publishing the seventh volume of her autobiography in 2013 at age 85.

A. Seven
B. Fourteen
C. Fifty
D. Eighty-six

18. Which of the following questions is directly answered by the passage?

Find and read in full context: Lines 70–73

S *Angelou returned to the American South in the 1980s to come to terms with her life there; she spent decades as a professor at Wake Forest University in Winston-Salem, North Carolina.*

F. What accomplishment was Angelou most proud of?
G. At what university was Angelou a professor?
H. What was the name of Angelou's son?
J. What year was Angelou's first novel published?

19. Based on the passage, Marguerite Annie Johnson chose to go by Maya Angelou because:

Find and read in full context: Lines 34–37

S *She took on the name Maya Angelou as a stage name of sorts, Maya coming from her childhood nickname and Angelou from Angelos, her former married surname.*

A. she wanted to honor her family with a stage name that referenced her father's name, Angelos.
B. as a touring performer, she required a stage name.
C. she wanted to honor the nickname given to her by Martha Graham and Alvin Ailey.
D. the name referenced a childhood nickname and her ex-husband's last name.

20. Maya Angelou's involvement in the civil rights movement:

Skim the First Paragraph: Lines 60–68

> *Activism in the civil rights movement was core to Angelou's life. Her relationship with South African freedom fighter Vusumzi Make took her to Cairo, and she later moved to Accra, Ghana. There, she met Malcolm X; in 1965, she returned to the United States to help create a new civil rights organization. She witnessed the LA riots in 1965 and continued the fight when she agreed to organize a march for Dr. Martin Luther King Jr. in 1968.*

F. inspired her to create a new civil rights organization based in Cairo and Ghana.
G. was an integral part of her life, especially as she became older.
H. led her to work with Martin Luther King, Jr. to create a documentary series.
J. motivated her to write a celebrated novel about the connection between Black American heritage and blues music.

Chapter 4

The Toolbox

Key Topics
- Passage Strategies
- Reordering the Passages
- The Read
- Timing
- Question Strategies
- Reordering Questions
- Process of Elimination
- Guessing Strategies

What's the Toolbox? Sounds exciting.
The Toolbox is a set of strategies to help you master the ACT Reading section as a *savvy test-taker*. Remember, you are learning how to play a game: the goal is to gain as many points as possible. In Chapters 2 and 3, you focused on building and improving your skills as a reader. In this chapter, you'll focus on building and improving your skills as a test-taker. The Toolbox is split into two compartments:

- Passage Strategies
- Question Strategies

Having the right tools in your Toolbox will help you feel more in control.

It's true: nothing beats close, careful reading. But the ACT is a very specific and very predictable test. Good reading on the ACT will look different from good reading in English class or at home. Some of these strategies might feel odd at first, but you'll get used to them with some practice.

Why should I use these strategies?
Both the Passage Strategies and the Question Strategies will help you with essential test-taking skills:

- Comprehension: making sure you understand the passages
- Timing: getting through the section within the time limits
- Comfort level: working through the section in a way that plays to your strengths

4.1 Passage Strategies

4.1.1 Reordering the Passages

Guess what? You don't need to complete the passages in order! Rearranging the passages can help you beat the clock and maximize correct answers. The passages on the ACT Reading section always appear in the same order:

1. Literary Narrative
2. Social Science
3. Humanities
4. Natural Science

As you practice, try starting and ending with different passages to find what works best for you.

How do I do that? There are three common options for reordering passages:

- **Save the Best for Last**

  One of the most popular rearrangements is to save the passage type you are most comfortable with for the end. That way, even if you are pressed for time, you can feel confident knowing that you're likely to quickly comprehend this last passage.

  Natural Science is often friendliest to complete last because you can pick up points quickly without closely reading the whole passage. Natural Science tends to have the most questions with clear locators, as well as a high number of Specific Detail questions.

- **Save the Worst for Last**

  Alternatively, if you are having trouble getting through all of the passages in time, you may want to leave your least favorite passage type for last. This will allow you to maximize your performance on the first three passages, the ones with which you are most comfortable. With whatever time you have left, pick up as many points as you can. (It's possible you may need to skip straight to the questions—more on that in the Question Strategies part of this chapter).

- **Save the Paired Passage for Last**

  Finally, you may find it helpful to save the Paired Passage for last, regardless of which genre it is. That way, if you're pressed for time, you can at least try to complete the reading and questions for one of the passages before guessing on the rest.

4.1.2 The Read

You don't have to read everything! On the ACT Reading section, strategic reading is more important than comprehensive reading. As we saw in Chapter 2, a good read should illuminate the theme and tone of a passage. But that doesn't necessarily mean you have to read the whole thing!

So, what are some different reading methods?
There are three popular ways to read the passages. You may use the same method for each passage, or you might try to mix it up based on passage type.

Here's an overview of the options. Keep reading for more specific instructions!

	Ideal Reading Time Per Passage	Works Well With...	Method
Read–It–All	3 minutes or less	Literary Narrative	Read the whole passage
Outline Method	2 minutes or less	Natural Science & Social Science	Read the entire introduction paragraph, topic sentence of each body paragraph, and the entire conclusion paragraph
2/3 Method	3 minutes or less	Humanities & Literary Narrative	Read the first column and the conclusion paragraph

Whichever reading method you choose, reading the conclusion paragraph is always essential! It often summarizes the author's primary argument and explains its significance.

- **Read–It–All**

  Simply put, you read the entire passage. Most students who go for the Read-It-All Method try to complete their readings in about 3 minutes or less. The 3 minute time limit is not a law, but it is a good rule of thumb to ensure you have enough time to tackle the questions.

  This can be a great approach if you're an especially fast reader, but don't worry if you can't get through every passage in 3 minutes! Some students find that reading the whole passage may not be worth the time. Others find that they get lost in the details of complex passages and can actually get the main idea more accurately by the Outline or 2/3 Method.

- **Outline Method**

  With this method, you outline the passage instead of reading the whole thing. You can often get a solid understanding of the passage's theme and tone by using the Outline Method. In addition, you'll get a general sense of where information is located, so you can find answers more quickly.

  How does the Outline Method work?

  You read three things:

  - The introduction paragraph
  - The topic sentences of each body paragraph
  - The conclusion paragraph

  If you choose the Outline Method for a passage, you should try to complete your read in 2 minutes or less.

Don't Forget: It may take more than the topic sentence to understand the main subject of a paragraph. Don't be afraid to read the second sentence, too, if you need to know a little more. Your goal is to get an outline of the author's main argument.

This sentence doesn't tell us much. Let's read on!

Example: This experiment led the scientists to a major discovery. The researchers found that the CRISPR editing technique successfully deleted the unwanted gene from a human embryo.

Try it! Read the following paired passage. Only the Outline is shown. If timing yourself, note that paired passages require half the reading time of a standard passage.

Passage IV

NATURAL SCIENCE: Passage A is adapted from the article "Pluto Downsized" by Ray Turner. (©2018 by Ray Turner).

Much to the dismay of many amateur astronomers, on August 24, 2006, the General Assembly of the International Astronomical Union (IAU) voted to demote Pluto from "planet" to "dwarf planet."

At the start of that year's deliberations, it had looked as though Pluto was going to be allowed to keep its title.

However, by week's end, astronomers (perhaps feeling their standards had become too lenient) added another, stricter, prerequisite: a planet also needs to be the most massive object in its orbital zone.

Though 424 astronomers voted on the resolution, their number represents a small fraction of the scientific community affected by the decision. Many scientists were not happy about the outcome.

Scientists assumed that low voting participation partially came from the lack of clarity around defining a "dwarf planet."

Much of the public holds a soft spot for Pluto, the underdog planet whose Disney namesake wasn't enough to save it. Online petitions and spirited debates were (45) sparked around the world following the IAU's declaration in an attempt to reinstate the beloved icy body as a planet. It seemed as though many took personal offense to its downgrade. The debate over Pluto's status captured the hearts and minds of many, a rare event in the realm of (50) astronomical nomenclature. And the American Dialect Society's 2006 Word of the Year? "Plutoed."

Even though you didn't read the whole passage, you should still be able to answer the following question:

1. Which of the following most accurately characterizes the main idea of the passage?

A. The General Assembly of the International Astronomical Union fought to keep Pluto classified as a planet.
B. To the dismay of some, changes in criteria resulted in the reclassification of a celestial body.
C. The planet Pluto was named after a Disney character.
D. Pluto was classified as a dwarf planet in the late 1990s by a group of 424 astronomers.

It's important to look out for distracting key phrases in the answer choices that might tempt you into choosing a wrong answer. In Chapter 2, you learned how to read your answer choices just as critically as you read the passage itself—if one detail is wrong, the entire answer choice is wrong. Even though answer choice B does not explicitly mention Pluto being renamed a dwarf planet, its general language is a correct paraphrase of exactly that main idea. The other answer choices do not summarize the passage's primary argument, and they each contain an error in a specific detail.

- **2/3 Method**

  If the Outline Method feels too brief but the Read–It–All Method takes too long, the 2/3 Method can be a nice compromise. Read the first half of the passage, then the conclusion paragraph, skipping over the other few paragraphs in between. One nice trick to keep in mind: if a question mentions some name or fact you don't remember reading, it will probably be located in the block of text that you skipped. You'll know exactly where to look for the answer.

  If you choose the 2/3 Method for a passage, aim to complete your read in 3 minutes or less.

Try it! Try out the 2/3 Method on Passage B, which is taken from the same paired passage. If you're timing yourself, remember that the paired passage requires half the reading time of a standard passage.

Passage IV

NATURAL SCIENCE: Passage B is adapted from the article "Dwarf Planets" by Jenna Cooper (©2017 by Jenna Cooper).

On the solar system's outskirts, way beyond Neptune, a collection of frozen objects swirls. Known as the Kuiper Belt, this icy region contains more than a thousand known giant entities, each greater than 62 miles (5) in diameter (though scientists predict there could be as many as 100,000 KBOs—Kuiper Belt Objects—in all). The KBOs are simply the remnants of debris that resulted from the chaotic formation of the solar system (mainly frozen volatiles like water, methane, and ammo- (10) nia), though the largest one was once, incredibly, widely known as our solar system's ninth planet: Pluto.

Today, Pluto is known as a dwarf planet. It has many properties similar to those of full-fledged planets, but it is much smaller. In fact, Pluto's diameter could barely (15) stretch halfway across the United States; it is smaller even than the earth's moon. Pluto also suffers something of an off-kilter orbit, another disqualification from planetary status. While the eight planets of the solar system (Mercury, Venus, Earth, Mars, Jupiter, Saturn, Uranus, (20) and Neptune) all orbit the sun in a near circle, Pluto's orbit is shaped more like a tilted oval, and the sun is not even at its center!

"It's wild to think that even just last year, we still had (45) no concrete idea of what Pluto's environment consisted of," said Matt Maroney, a New Horizons project scientist. "But it didn't take long for us to realize Pluto was incredibly unique, far more so than we ever could have expected. We've been surprised not only by the planet's complexity, (50) but also by its beauty. I can say we're absolutely looking forward to the discoveries still ahead of us."

Again, even though you didn't read the whole passage, you should still be able to answer the following question:

2. Which of the following most accurately characterizes the main idea of the passage?

F. Pluto is an unexpectedly cold dwarf planet, with temperatures averaging –375 degrees Fahrenheit.
G. Some Kuiper Belt Objects are actually dwarf planets, the largest of which is Pluto.
H. Scientists continue to learn surprising facts about Pluto, the largest of the Kuiper Belt Objects.
J. Pluto is too complex to be classified only as a dwarf planet.

Because you are looking for the main idea of the passage, don't allow yourself to get distracted by specific details. You need an answer choice that encompasses what the entire passage is about, not just one paragraph. Passage B is concerned with listing facts about Pluto, including details about how those facts were discovered, making H the best answer.

Now that you understand the main idea of both paired passages, you can answer comparative questions like the one below:

3. Which of the following statements best compares the way the authors of Passage A and Passage B categorize Pluto?

A. Passage A states that Pluto was classified as a dwarf planet after a period of intense scientific debate, and Passage B states that Pluto was classified as a dwarf planet due to its small size and tilted orbit.
B. Passage A categorizes Pluto as a planet despite the International Astronomical Union's attempts to categorize it as a dwarf planet, while Passage B categorizes Pluto as a planet because it shares so many qualities with similar celestial bodies.
C. Both Passage A and Passage B categorize Pluto as a planet, despite recent attempts by the International Astronomical Union to demote Pluto to a dwarf planet.
D. Both Passage A and Passage B categorize Pluto as a dwarf planet, even though the New Horizons spacecraft recently gathered data that may force scientists to reclassify Pluto as a planet.

In order to answer this question, it is important to make sure that you are keeping track of which specific details are related to which passage. You can use process of elimination by proving (or disproving, as the case may be) the Passage A portion of the answer choices first. This eliminates B and C since Passage A ultimately categorizes Pluto as a dwarf planet. Now you are left with answer choices A and D. Even though both passages state that Pluto is classified as a dwarf planet, Passage A doesn't mention the New Horizons spacecraft (and even though Passage B does, the data from New Horizons isn't giving scientists a reason to change their classification). As a result, we are left with A, which we can prove with evidence from both texts.

One of the passages on the ACT Reading section will always be a Paired Passage with a Passage A and a Passage B. The questions are broken up by passage, so make sure to use that to your advantage! When you see paired passages...

1. **Read Passage A, then complete Passage A questions.**
2. **Read Passage B, then complete Passage B questions.**
3. **Complete the questions that have to do with comparing and contrasting the two passages.**

All of the same strategies from this chapter still apply to the Paired Passage.

4.1.3 Timing

The goal of any timing strategy[1] is not just to maximize the number of questions you answer but the number of questions you answer *correctly*. The following timing breakdowns will help you to distribute your 35 minutes strategically across the four passages. As you choose the breakdown that works for you, keep in mind that you should NEVER sacrifice accuracy for speed. Instead, choose the timing strategy that allows you to work at a comfortable (but efficient) pace. You will earn a higher score if you work at a pace that allows you to answer questions correctly, not a pace that forces you to rush to get to every question.

Here are the most common timing breakdowns, any of which can earn you a good reading score:

1. 9, 9, 9, 8 minutes: If you're comfortable moving at a quick pace, you can devote an almost-equal amount of time to each passage and complete the section.
2. 11, 8, 8, 8 minutes: If you need more time to comprehend one of the passage types (Literary Narrative, for example), give yourself 11 minutes there. Then, work a bit more quickly on the remaining three.
3. 10, 10, 10, 5 minutes: This is a common starting point for a lot of students. Allowing 10 minutes per passage can help you maximize reading comprehension. It's true: the last passage will be a bit of a rush. But that's okay. To help, do an Outline Read of the last passage or skip straight to the questions.
4. 11, 11, 11, 2 minutes: You always want to work at a comfortable pace. If that means you need 11 minutes per passage, use the 11 minutes. With this timing method, you will be rushing through the last passage. But what's most important is that you'll be comfortable on the first 3 passages. For the last passage, just skip straight to the questions.

No matter which timing strategy you use, remember to ALWAYS bubble in an answer for every single question. The ACT does not take points off for incorrect answers, so even random guesses can earn you extra points. If you are bubbling in random guesses for a few questions in a row, stick to the same letter—for example, bubble in B/G for the last 3 that you didn't have time for.

Try it! As you've read, there are 3 variables to play around with: Passage Order, Reading Method, and Timing. The only way to figure out which methods work best for you is to experiment. Use the table on the following page to record your reading method, reading speed, and the order in which you read the passages in this book. You can use the test at the end of this chapter and the 3 Practice Tests at the end of this book. You can also record your accuracy. How many minutes do you need to answer questions accurately? Does outlining the passage work better than reading the whole thing? As you experiment, you'll discover which types of passages you like best, which you like least, which you read fastest, and which you read slowest. The important thing is to find the timing, the reading method, and the passage order that work for you. Stick to it on test day!

[1]If you have accommodations that grant extended time, check out page 151 for more information.

Passage Order	Accuracy	Speed	Reading Methods Used
Chapter 4 Test 1. 2. 3. 4.	1. ___ /10 2. ___ /10 3. ___ /10 4. ___ /10 **Total: ___ /40**	1. ___ minutes 2. ___ minutes 3. ___ minutes 4. ___ minutes	
Practice Test 1 1. 2. 3. 4.	1. ___ /10 2. ___ /10 3. ___ /10 4. ___ /10 **Total: ___ /40**	1. ___ minutes 2. ___ minutes 3. ___ minutes 4. ___ minutes	
Practice Test 2 1. 2. 3. 4.	1. ___ /10 2. ___ /10 3. ___ /10 4. ___ /10 **Total: ___ /40**	1. ___ minutes 2. ___ minutes 3. ___ minutes 4. ___ minutes	
Practice Test 3 1. 2. 3. 4.	1. ___ /10 2. ___ /10 3. ___ /10 4. ___ /10 **Total: ___ /40**	1. ___ minutes 2. ___ minutes 3. ___ minutes 4. ___ minutes	

4.2 Question Strategies

4.2.1 Reordering Questions

I get that I can reorder the passages—but I have to do the questions in order, right?

Nope! ACT Reading questions aren't arranged in order of difficulty, meaning they don't go from easy to hard. They also don't follow the sequence of the passage, meaning the first questions don't necessarily refer to the beginning of the passage and the last questions don't necessarily refer to the end of the passage. Because they are organized randomly, doing the questions in order isn't very efficient.

As a result, reordering questions is one of the most powerful strategies you can use. Skipping to answer the fast questions first allows you to (1) never waste time searching for hard-to-find details and (2) build a stronger understanding of the passage's organization and main ideas so that when you get to the harder questions, you know where to find the answers.

So...how exactly should I reorder them? → just a fancy word for levels!

We can organize questions into **three different tiers** based on how quickly the answer can be found. Following these guidelines for re-ordering questions will help you strategically manage your time and strengthen your passage comprehension!

- **Tier 1:** First, complete any questions that tell you exactly where to look by giving you clear locators that you can find quickly:
  - Line Numbers
  - Specific Paragraphs

As a bonus, doing questions with clear locators first will help you review a large chunk of the text before approaching questions with tougher-to-find answers.

Here are some examples of Tier 1 questions: → No need to answer these! Just notice how the questions are worded for each tier.

1. In line 58 of Passage B, the term "KBOs" most accurately refers to:

A. planetary objects located between Neptune and the Earth.
B. frozen bodies located in the solar system beyond Neptune.
C. remnants of the solar system's formation composed mainly of debris from nearby planet Pluto.
D. Neptune and its surrounding planetary objects.

2. In Passage A, the primary purpose of the first paragraph is to:

   F. explain a controversial decision made by the General Assembly of the International Astronomical Union.
   G. argue that Pluto should not have been declassified as a planet.
   H. summarize the key reasons for a critical decision made about Pluto's planetary status.
   J. introduce the main subject of an ongoing debate.

Game Changer! **Tier 1 questions are also fantastic options when you're low on time! If you are using the 10, 10, 10, 5 or 11, 11, 11, 2 timing strategy, you should skip directly to Tier 1 questions for your 5 or 2 minute passage.**

- **Tier 2:** Once you've answered the Tier 1 questions, complete all questions that do **not** contain words in ALL CAPITAL LETTERS and that do not ask you about the chronological order of events. Hopefully, doing the Tier 1 questions has helped you to better map out where the key information is located in the passage.

→ Tier 2 = everything that is NOT Tier 1 or Tier 3

Here are some examples of Tier 2 questions:

1. In Passage A, it can most reasonably be inferred that scientists would agree about which of the following statements?

   A. The decision to declassify Pluto as a planet has been a controversial one.
   B. Pluto should be classified as a dwarf planet due to its irregular orbit.
   C. Planets must meet universal requirements for mass, orbit, and roundness.
   D. Public petitions should not influence the classification of planetary objects.

2. The main purpose of Passage B is to:

   F. summarize some key findings and current research topics about the planet Pluto.
   G. explain the pros and cons of classifying Pluto as a dwarf planet.
   H. explore the significance of the Kuiper Belt Objects, including the planet Pluto.
   J. summarize some key characteristics of Kuiper Belt Objects.

3. According to Passage B, the New Horizons spacecraft was launched in order to:

   A. gather additional information about Pluto.
   B. verify Pluto's status as a Kuiper Belt Object.
   C. investigate the environmental factors contributing to Pluto's extreme atmosphere and temperature.
   D. investigate the solar system beyond the Kuiper Belt.

Game Changer! **Questions that contain easy-to-find locators (like capitalized proper nouns, and numbers) often have answers that are easier to locate in the passage. Try completing those questions before ones with less clear locators!**

- **Tier 3:** Finally, answer the questions with words containing **ALL CAPITAL LETTERS** (LEAST/NOT/EXCEPT) and questions that ask about the **chronological order of events**. These questions tend to take the most time since they ask you to locate multiple pieces of information in multiple locations.

Here are some examples of Tier 3 questions:

1. According to Passage A, which of the following is NOT a requirement for the classification of a planetary object as a true planet?

A. Roundness
B. Mass
C. Solar distance
D. Regular orbit

2. In Passage A, which of the following happened first chronologically?

F. Scientists stated that a planet must be the most massive object in its orbital zone.
G. The public signed petitions in support of Pluto's planetary status.
H. The Planetary assembly of the IAU voted to classify Pluto as a dwarf planet.
J. The Planetary Definition Committee stated that planets would be defined as round objects in orbit around the sun.

Try it! On the next page are the full versions of the two passages you've read using the Outline and 2/3 Method. First, practice categorizing the questions by Tier. Then answer the questions in order from Tier 1 to Tier 2 to Tier 3. Remember: use your Paired Passage reading strategy!

Passage IV

NATURAL SCIENCE: Passage A is adapted from the article "Pluto Downsized" by Ray Turner. (©2018 by Ray Turner). Passage B is adapted from the article "Dwarf Planets" by Jenna Cooper (©2017 by Jenna Cooper).

Passage A by Ray Turner

Much to the dismay of many amateur astronomers, on August 24, 2006, the General Assembly of the International Astronomical Union (IAU) voted to demote Pluto from "planet" to "dwarf planet."

5 At the start of that year's deliberations, it had looked as though Pluto was going to be allowed to keep its title. On August 16, after a full year of meetings, the Planet Definition Committee (yes, that's really what it's called) stated that planets were to be defined as spheroidal objects 10 orbiting the Sun. Roundness was a crucial factor because it signified hydrostatic equilibrium—a celestial body's balance between its internal pressure pushing outward and the gravitational forces pulling matter inward. For one ecstatic week, this definition not only included 15 Pluto, but actually would have added another three entities to the official solar system!

However, by week's end, astronomers (perhaps feeling their standards had become too lenient) added another, stricter, prerequisite: a planet also needs to be the 20 most massive object in its orbital zone. Not only did this disqualify the three potential new planets, it left Pluto out in the cold as well. Pluto's strange secret has always been that there are thousands of other icy bodies in the outer Solar System where it orbits, some larger than Pluto it- 25 self. As a result, Pluto was reclassified: dwarf planet.

Though 424 astronomers voted on the resolution, their number represents a small fraction of the scientific community affected by the decision. Many scientists were not happy about the outcome. "I'm embarrassed 30 for astronomy," said Richard Humphrey, an astronomer at the Northwest Research Institute. "Less than 5 percent of the world's astronomers voted."

Scientists assumed that low voting participation partially came from the lack of clarity around defining a 35 "dwarf planet." The official language reads that a dwarf planet is any spheroidal object that "has not cleared the neighborhood around its orbit, and is not a satellite." Plutophiles pushed back that other planets orbit alongside asteroids, meaning their orbit is not "clear." Even those 40 supportive of the IAU's decision to declassify Pluto questioned the language used to do so.

Much of the public holds a soft spot for Pluto, the underdog planet whose Disney namesake wasn't enough to save it. Online petitions and spirited debates were 45 sparked around the world following the IAU's declaration in an attempt to reinstate the beloved icy body as a planet. It seemed as though many took personal offense to its downgrade. The debate over Pluto's status captured the hearts and minds of many, a rare event in the realm of 50 astronomical nomenclature. And the American Dialect Society's 2006 Word of the Year? "Plutoed."

Passage B by Jenna Cooper

On the solar system's outskirts, way beyond Neptune, a collection of frozen objects swirls. Known as the Kuiper Belt, this icy region contains more than a thou- 55 sand known giant entities, each greater than 62 miles in diameter (though scientists predict there could be as many as 100,000 KBOs—Kuiper Belt Objects—in all.) The KBOs are simply the remnants of debris that resulted from the chaotic formation of the solar system 60 (mainly frozen volatiles like water, methane, and ammonia), though the largest one was once, incredibly, widely known as our solar system's ninth planet: Pluto.

Today, Pluto is known as a dwarf planet. It has many properties similar to those of full-fledged planets, but it 65 is much smaller. In fact, Pluto's diameter could barely stretch halfway across the United States; it is smaller even than the earth's moon. Pluto also suffers something of an off–kilter orbit, another disqualification from planetary status. While the eight planets of the solar system 70 (Mercury, Venus, Earth, Mars, Jupiter, Saturn, Uranus, and Neptune) all orbit the sun in a near circle, Pluto's orbit is shaped more like a tilted oval, and the sun is not even at its center!

As for the dwarf planet's ground conditions, our 75 far distant neighbor resembles our outer planets. The weather on Pluto is incredibly cold: typically, the temperature dips down to –375 degrees Fahrenheit. With those temperatures, Earth's air would freeze into a strange snow composed not only of water, but of every element 80 that comprises our atmosphere. When it was classified as a planet, Pluto had the distinction of being the coldest of the nine; now that honor belongs to Uranus (though Neptune, the other "ice giant," comes in a close second).

Perhaps unsurprisingly, declassification has not at 85 all curbed fascination or thwarted exploration of Pluto. In January 2006, NASA launched a spacecraft named New Horizons to fly to Pluto. Although the craft could have flown from Los Angeles to New York in four minutes, to traverse the enormous distance between Earth and Pluto 90 took New Horizons nearly ten years. Finally, in the summer of 2015, three billion miles from take-off, New Horizons' cameras and spectrometers sent their first stream of data to NASA.

"It's wild to think that even just last year, we still had 95 no concrete idea of what Pluto's environment consisted of," said Matt Maroney, New Horizons project scientist. "But it didn't take long for us to realize Pluto was incredibly unique, far more so than we ever could have expected. We've been surprised not only by the planet's complexity, 100 but also by its beauty. I can say we're absolutely looking forward to the discoveries still ahead of us."

Questions 1–4 ask about Passage A.

1. _____ In the context of Passage A, the main purpose of the third paragraph (lines 17–25) is to:

A. transition from the description of a likely outcome to a statement of what actually occurred.
B. illustrate the reasons for the public's displeasure with Pluto's new status.
C. provide data about Pluto's size in comparison to other icy bodies in the region.
D. clarify the author's opinion that Pluto should have been considered a planet instead of a dwarf planet.

2. _____ Passage A makes clear that people were upset about Pluto's downgraded status for all of the following reasons EXCEPT:

F. people have a soft spot for Pluto, which reminds them of a Disney character.
G. a majority of astronomers did not vote to make the decision.
H. the definition of a dwarf planet is ambiguous.
J. astronomers believe that Pluto fits the definition of roundness due to its hydrostatic equilibrium.

3. _____ It can reasonably be inferred from Passage A that if Pluto had ultimately been defined as a planet:

A. no astronomers would have agreed with the decision by the Planet Definition Committee.
B. the other planets in the solar system would have then been under scrutiny.
C. much of the public still would have been upset with the classification.
D. three similar bodies would also have been classified as planets.

4. _____ The main idea of the last paragraph of Passage A is that the general public:

F. decided to become astronomers to have more say in decisions about planets.
G. protested vehemently against the International Astronomical Union.
H. recognized the astronomers' expertise and respected the decision.
J. had an emotional reaction and wanted to overturn Pluto's change in status.

Questions 5–7 ask about Passage B.

5. _____ According to Passage B, Pluto's size is approximately equal to:

A. half the width of the United States.
B. the radius of Uranus.
C. the diameter of Earth's moon.
D. the circumference of Neptune.

6. _____ In Passage B, the primary purpose of the statement in lines 77–80 is to:

F. demonstrate astronomers' lack of understanding about Pluto.
G. illustrate the intensity of the cold temperatures on Pluto.
H. explain why humans would not be able to live on Pluto.
J. reveal similarities between Pluto and planets like Uranus and Neptune.

7. _____ The first paragraph most strongly suggests that the number of significant icy bodies in the Kuiper Belt is predicted to be:

A. 62.
B. 500.
C. between 1,000 and 100,000.
D. greater than 100,000.

Questions 8–10 ask about both passages.

8. _____ Which of the following best compares details about Pluto's orbit as they are used by the two authors?

F. Both passages clearly state that Pluto's orbit is shaped like an oval.
G. Both passages indicate that the shape of Pluto's orbit is irrelevant to its status as a planet.
H. Passage A implies that Pluto orbits around the Sun, while Passage B states that the Sun is not the center of Pluto's orbit.
J. Passage A focuses on other icy bodies, while Passage B demonstrates that Pluto is the only icy body of its type.

9. _____ Both passages suggest that one of the features that makes Pluto a dwarf planet is its:

A. great distance from the sun.
B. hydrostatic equilibrium that causes it to be round.
C. categorization as a KBO.
D. size.

10. _____ The passages are most similar in their use of:

F. contrast words to illustrate a debate.
G. statistics to describe Pluto.
H. quotations to indicate scientists' reactions.
J. occasional first person point of view.

Answer Key

1. A — Tier 1
2. J — Tier 3
3. D — Tier 2
4. J — Tier 1
5. A — Tier 2
6. G — Tier 1
7. C — Tier 1
8. H — Tier 2
9. D — Tier 2
10. H — Tier 2

Now that you've learned how to categorize questions by Tier, it's time to learn some strategies for answering them!

4.2.2 Process of Elimination

Once you are reading with good focus and comprehension, use the ACT's multiple choice format to your advantage. The ACT has clear patterns that often distinguish correct answers from incorrect answers. Identifying and using those patterns to maximize points is what process of elimination is all about.

But what if I'm just not that great at multiple choice exams?
That's okay. A few basic tips and common traps to watch out for will help you see that multiple choice really is a gift, as long as you know how to work it. Here are some important points for saving time and avoiding multiple choice traps:

Confused about anticipating answers? Check out Chapter 3 - Question Categories!

- Always try to **anticipate** first. Don't dive straight into process of elimination. This might sound like a counter-intuitive point to make in a section about process of elimination, but it's true: the first rule of process of elimination is to avoid process of elimination as a first course of action. Instead, think of your own answer first, and base it on what you've read in the passage. By answering the question in your own words, you will be able to go into the answer choices confidently, looking for what you know to be correct. Additionally, you'll avoid two common traps:
  - You won't be as likely to fall for "cut and paste" answers that contain a memorable phrase from the passage but don't actually answer the question at hand.
  - You won't fall for well-worded answers that are close but wrong. The ACT Reading section often tempts you with intelligent-sounding answers that can throw you off track if you don't anticipate ("Oh! I wasn't thinking of the passage in that way, but maybe that's what they actually meant!")
- But...sometimes you won't be able to anticipate an answer. Some ACT questions are too open-ended, or just too difficult. For example, a question might ask something like "Which of the following questions is most clearly answered in the passage?" In this case, you can't anticipate the answer because you don't know what follows. When you encounter questions you can't anticipate an answer for, go straight to the answer choices. Skim to see what kinds of answers you're looking for in the text. Then proceed as usual.

Now it's time to try out Process of Elimination!

- **Keep Your Pencil Moving:** Create your own code for when to keep or get rid of an answer choice. For example, you could use an "x" mark for answers you eliminate and a dash for answers you want to mark as a "maybe." It doesn't matter which specific marks you choose; the important thing is to keep it consistent and easy to remember.

3. According to Passage B, Pluto's size is approximately equal to:

A. half the width of the United States.
B. the radius of Uranus.
C. the diameter of Earth's moon.
D. the circumference of Neptune.

- **Maintain Strict Rules:** Know exactly when you are allowed to get rid of a possible answer choice. You cannot eliminate an answer until you KNOW it is wrong. If you have a feeling that it's wrong, but have no evidence, do not eliminate the answer.

4. The main idea of the last paragraph of Passage A is that the general public:

F. decided to become astronomers to have more say in decisions about planets.
G. protested vehemently against the International Astronomical Union.
H. recognized the astronomers' expertise and respected the decision.
J. had an emotional reaction and wanted to overturn Pluto's change in status.

Don't Forget: If you don't know the definition of a word, that doesn't mean you can eliminate it! Don't be afraid to pick an answer choice that includes a word you haven't seen before—if you can prove that the other three answers are definitely wrong, then the right answer has to be the one with the unfamiliar vocab word. On the other hand, if one of the choices that you do understand completely seems correct, you can feel free to choose that answer and eliminate the one with the unfamiliar word.

4.2.3 Guessing Strategies

Can't you just tell me which answer choices are correct?
Actually...kind of!

You can get really good at spotting "good-looking" and "bad-looking" answer choices. That's because the ACT Reading section has a habit of favoring certain kinds of answer choices over others. The following tips are guidelines, not hard and fast rules. But they can be surprisingly helpful in eliminating incorrect answers.

- Test the Twins: If two answer choices are more similar to one another than they are to the other answer choices, the correct answer is likely one of those two! Look for the key differences between them to decide which one is accurate and which one is *slightly* incorrect. Here's an example:

  5. The primary function of the third paragraph is to:

  A. explain how previous studies questioned the **theory's validity.**
  B. dispute all previous claims of the **theory's validity.**
  C. completely validate Miriam's hunch about hyperactive nuclei.
  D. provide exposition necessary to fully comprehend every technical nuance.

  Both answer choices A and B address the "theory's validity," suggesting that the answer choice is likely one of those two options. Even if you can't ultimately decide between these two, at least now you've got a 50/50 shot!

- The Nothing Answer: Answer choices that are more **moderate, general, nuanced** and **balanced** than the other answer choices tend to be correct. Take a look at the following example:

6. The primary function of the third paragraph is to:

F. explain how previous studies questioned the theory's validity.
G. dispute all previous claims of the theory's validity.
H. completely validate Miriam's hunch about hyperactive nuclei.
J. provide exposition necessary to fully comprehend every technical nuance.

  - If G were the correct answer, the text would have to prove that every single claim was disputed—which it probably doesn't.
  - If H were correct, the text would have to completely prove her hunch correct, and that hunch would have to be specifically about "hyperactive nuclei." Having a specific subject opens up room for inaccuracy—maybe her hunch was about something else!
  - If J were correct, the passage would have to completely explain each and every "technical nuance"—which, again, the passage probably does not do.
  - Finally, when compared to the other answer choices, F is the most general, moderate answer choice—and therefore the most likely to be correct. And it is, in fact, the correct answer choice!

When should I use these Guessing Strategies?

Here are four situations in which these strategies can be especially helpful:

- When you're stuck between two answer choices
- To give you more confidence on the answer you've already chosen
- During the first pass read of each answer choice
- When you're in a time-crunch and need to make some quick guesses

Try it! On the following page, choose answers to the questions without their respective passages by using the Guessing Strategies. Although it may feel counterintuitive to answer questions without having read their passages first, strategic guessing in an important ACT skill to practice! Test the Twins, spot the Nothing Answers, and be wary of extreme and specific answers.

1. Based on the passage, it could be assumed the narrator acquired the knowledge to tell this story about Forest by:

A. piecing the information together from the awful stories she had heard.
B. interviewing friends, family and acquaintances of Forest before their camp session had ended.
C. participating in activities as they occurred.
D. never forgetting a single detail as Forest relayed stories.

2. In the context of Passage A, the author most likely uses the description of a melted candle (lines 15–16) to:

F. illustrate the manner in which they responded.
G. exemplify the caliber of academic excellence the class exuded.
H. contradict the teacher's bizarre pedagogy.
J. contextualize the theories of Constance, Grange, and Whittle.

3. To support claims regarding science fiction's influence on celebrity culture, the author utilizes:

A. statistical analysis of Dr. Feinstein's recorded data.
B. definitions of every classification currently available.
C. examples illustrating the three leading theories.
D. quotations from experts in the field.

4. According to the Bastian, he might have become "much improved" (line 23) if he had:

F. maintained the callous demeanor he fostered at sleepaway camp.
G. equated his time in school to that of his brother, Larry's.
H. mastered the extremely biased plan his mother had set out for him.
J. questioned the somewhat controversial plan his mother had set out for him.

5. The overall organization of the passage is best described as a:

A. step-by-step analysis of the calculations used to describe variances in price.
B. series of mundane and overtly funny anecdotes relating to Joshua Tree.
C. collection of stories illustrating why nobody travels to Joshua Tree.
D. summary of various existing theories pertaining to the debated topic.

6. Within Passage B, the image in lines 42–46 functions figuratively to suggest that:

F. Dane's sadness about the swimming conditions had irreversibly changed his mood.
G. The calm nature of the day was only a product of their natural surroundings.
H. Anita's swimming under a full moon was shocking, given her relationship with Dane.
J. Anita's swimming under a full moon was fitting, given the circumstances.

7. The primary purpose of the passage is to:

A. describe the evolution of research techniques used to discover and recreate dinosaur mandibles.
B. provide an overview of the the mechanics of the mandibles of certain species.
C. compare the mandibles of carnivorous dinosaurs to those of herbivores.
D. describe the process of Bane and Xavier's academic research.

8. The author most strongly implies that people commonly assume the most lush forests are:

F. contained within a fifteen mile radius of major cities.
G. farthest from the coasts of continents within the Northern Hemisphere.
H. within the general vicinity of a body of water.
J. located in the exact center of various continents.

9. The passage indicates that architects could not find a suitable alternative until:

A. scientists had rid the area of toxins like lead and nitrates.
B. permits had been obtained at both the state and federal levels.
C. they fabricated the world's largest compass.
D. the errors of previous attempts had been properly analyzed.

10. According to the passage, the frosting on Reina's birthday cake resembled:

F. details from her chemistry book, of which she had childhood memories.
G. aspects of the natural world with which she had a personal connection.
H. the world's most elaborate latticework.
J. unique designs she had crafted at age five.

Answer Key

1. Based on the passage, it could be assumed the narrator acquired the knowledge to tell this story about Forest by:

   A. piecing the information together from the awful stories she had heard.
   B. interviewing friends, family, and acquaintances of Forest before their camp session had ended.
   C. participating in activities as they occurred.
   D. never forgetting a single detail as Forest relayed stories.

2. In the context of Passage A, the author most likely uses the description of a melted candle (lines 15–16) to:

   F. illustrate the manner in which they responded.
   G. exemplify the caliber of academic excellence the class exuded.
   H. contradict the teacher's bizarre pedagogy.
   J. contextualize the theories of Constance, Grange, and Whittle.

3. To support claims regarding science fiction's influence on celebrity culture, the author utilizes:

   A. statistical analysis of Dr. Feinstein's recorded data.
   B. definitions of every classification currently available.
   C. examples illustrating the three leading theories.
   D. quotations from experts in the field.

4. According to the Bastian, he might have become "much improved" (line 23) if he had:

   F. maintained the callous demeanor he fostered at sleepaway camp.
   G. equated his time in school to that of his brother, Larry's.
   H. mastered the extremely biased plan his mother had set out for him.
   J. questioned the somewhat controversial plan his mother had set out for him.

5. The overall organization of the passage is best described as a:

   A. step-by-step analysis of the calculations used to describe variances in price.
   B. series of mundane and overtly funny anecdotes relating to Joshua Tree.
   C. collection of stories illustrating why nobody travels to Joshua Tree.
   D. summary of various existing theories pertaining to the debated topic.

6. Within Passage B, the image in lines 42–46 functions figuratively to suggest that:

   F. Dane's sadness about the swimming conditions had irreversibly changed his mood.
   G. The calm nature of the day was only a product of their natural surroundings.
   H. Anita's swimming under a full moon was shocking, given her relationship with Dane.
   J. Anita's swimming under a full moon was fitting, given the circumstances.

7. The primary purpose of the passage is to:

   A. describe the evolution of research techniques used to discover and recreate dinosaur mandibles.
   B. provide an overview of the the mechanics of the mandibles of certain species.
   C. compare the mandibles of carnivorous dinosaurs to those of herbivores.
   D. describe the process of Bane and Xavier's academic research.

8. The author most strongly implies that people commonly assume the most lush forests are:

   F. contained within a fifteen mile radius from major cities.
   G. farthest from the coasts of continents within the Northern Hemisphere.
   H. within the general vicinity of a body of water.
   J. located in the exact center of various continents.

9. The passage indicates that architects could not find a suitable alternative until:

   A. scientists had rid the area of toxins like lead and nitrates.
   B. permits had been obtained at both the state and federal levels.
   C. they fabricated the world's largest compass.
   D. the errors of previous attempts had been properly analyzed.

10. According to the passage, the frosting on Reina's birthday cake resembled:

    F. details from her chemistry book, of which she had childhood memories.
    G. aspects of the natural world with which she had a personal connection.
    H. the world's most elaborate lattice work.
    J. unique designs she had crafted at age five.

4.3 Chapter Test

Congratulations—You've completed Chapter 4! Just to recap, you should now have a general understanding of...

- Passage Strategies
  - Reordering Passages
  - The Read
  - Timing
- Question Strategies
  - Reordering Questions
  - Process of Elimination
  - Guessing Strategies

The Chapter Test on the following pages will test these skills. Use it as an opportunity to try out everything you've learned from this chapter as best you can. That requires coordinating a lot of moving pieces, so be patient with yourself and just do your best!

CHAPTER TEST

35 Minutes — 40 Questions

DIRECTIONS: There are four passages in this test. Each passage is followed by several questions. After reading a passage, choose the best answer to each question and fill in the corresponding oval on your answer document. You may refer to the passages as often as necessary.

Passage I

LITERARY NARRATIVE: This passage is adapted from the short story *Dog Days* by Bertha Zimmerman (©2018 by Zimmerman National Press).

Jason worked faster than Mike, and Mike worked faster than Paul, but Paul didn't work all that fast to begin with. So the pace of summer remained genial, the labor just brisk enough to appear unlazy. At the heart of 5 their idyll was the fact of the Gables' land, which at 135 acres might have appeared a sizeable property, daunting for three teenage boys to maintain alone, but aside from its small dock in the harbor and those cobble-y walks around the main house, the Gables was just a mass of pine 10 scrub and bramble. Very little actual maintenance was required. Sure, Jason might cut a wayward root, Paul a fallen limb. Mike might throw some gravel in a pot hole. But in fact the few paths that weaved through the property's heart were maintained almost entirely by their own 15 natural logic. It was as if, in conspiracy with the boys, the deer and rabbits and the rosehips and vines were the real groundskeepers of the inn.

And so, following the morning batch of chores—the dock scrub, the cosmetic clippings, the mowing, the in- 20 veterate slathering of white paint on shingles—the boys found ample time for idle afternoon sojourns into the forest, where in the name of trail work they would often disappear for hours. For Paul and Jason these outings were an awakening. It was as if only by exiting the manicured 25 grounds of the main house could they relax their public smiles and in the wilderness enact whatever their professions had concealed all morning. Mike, who foresaw the woods would come to hold all their memories of the year, dutifully spent much of his time in contemplation, as if 30 keeping a secret picture book for later use.

In either case, the woods were the boys' own. Though the Gables' paths led to various poorly-marketed landmarks, the wilderness went largely ignored by the Inn's disinterested guests, who, city-slickers all, pre- 35 ferred to sun at the pool or sit stone-like in the adirondack chairs by the dock, their leisure a perpetual convalescence. Thus it was in absolute freedom that Jason and Paul—racing from start to finish of Crooked Creek Path, launching from the rope swing at Sally's Pond, climb- 40 ing to the tops of the anemic pines—took over the entire landscape. They turned every conceivable minute into a running competition: no height, no distance, no speed went unrecorded. Mike, for his part, played the referee, the judge, the moderator. He dutifully recorded Jason's 45 4 second win over Paul, though he would not admit to his fundamental disinterest in the statistics. For what interested Mike was not recorded time, but time itself. It felt to him as though time had become untethered during those afternoons, was suspended between past and future. 50 So, he had a strange feeling that even as he stood on the banks of Sally's Pond, measuring the distance of Paul's jump from the rope swing, he was at the same time projecting backward from a future in which the moment of Paul's jump had already passed.

55 Mike was lost in one such thought when he watched Paul suddenly (on Jason's dare) scramble down the sheer bank of Peterman's Point. "And the second dare is to climb back up," shouted Jason, now staring in disbelief at the narrow beach where Paul, impossibly, appeared be- 60 low. "Simple!" Paul shouted up, before trying, and utterly failing, to find any purchase, any foothold, even any handhold to grasp in the sheer cliff face.

Mike stared down. It was an enormous cliff. No one could deny Paul his achievement. "I'd say one hundred 65 feet, at least," he said, a number Jason disputed, though conceded the cliff was high.

For some minutes they all admired the astonishing fact that Paul had actually done it. Certainly, it had never been done before in the entire history of The Gables. But 70 the sheer thoughtless will that had propelled Paul's descent now seemed to hold no sway whatsoever over his efforts to get back up. Mike scanned the scene for the possibility of some missing piece of information—some unseen path, or a shallow crossing to a less formidable 75 cliff of land—but The Point's minimalist beauty was unfortunately also Paul's prison. There was nothing but a rock cliff and waves stretching to the horizon. Paul, struggling with futile effort against the wall, finally called it a "muddle."

80 Mike and Jason leaned over the edge to talk. Paul, in inexplicable high spirits, straddled the two rocks that comprised his narrow beach. "Come on down," he called. "Bring some chairs." For a while they lay there. In three hours, Mike thought, the sun would set, and as it had ev- 85 ery day at The Gables, another work log would exaggerate their duties performed, and another morning would lead them closer to September. It had been a good season, he thought, maybe even great. Though he felt certain that greatness would take many years to know. Who could 90 tell whether if, in the gauzy reflection of nostalgia, this chunk of passing time would command any enduring appeal? In the meantime, he thought, they would somehow have to fish up Paul.

1. Which of the following best characterizes the boys' work ethic at The Gables?

A. Paul and Jason are slow workers, but Mike is able to work quickly.
B. Paul, Mike, and Jason are lazy and avoid their work.
C. The boys compete with one another to see who can work fastest.
D. The boys do enough work to fulfill their responsibilities but little more.

2. The tone of the story can best be described as:

F. comic and foreboding.
G. nostalgic and bittersweet.
H. critical and sarcastic.
J. droll and judgmental.

3. The story is told from which of the following points of view?

A. A young man looking back on his adolescence
B. An omniscient narrator who jumps between various times and various characters' thoughts
C. An omniscient narrator with close access to the thoughts of one character
D. A teenager relaying the events of his summer

4. The narrator makes use of all of the following EXCEPT:

F. rhetorical questions.
G. figurative language.
H. allusion to classical literature.
J. comic irony.

5. Which of the following does the passage directly compare?

A. The competitive personalities of Jason and Paul with the contemplative personality of Mike
B. The close friendship between Jason and Paul with Mike's isolated position in the group
C. Mike's nostalgia for the past with his fear of the future
D. Jason's athletic ability with Paul's bravery

6. In lines 25–26, the phrase "relax their public smiles" most nearly refers to:

F. the suffering Jason and Paul endure when forced to work at the main house.
G. the contrast between the guests' and the boys' manners.
H. the fear Jason and Paul have of the main house.
J. the freedom Jason and Paul feel when allowed to leave the area of the main house.

7. It can reasonably be inferred that the setting of the passage is:

A. a large luxury resort.
B. a spiritual retreat in the mountains.
C. an old Inn on the coast.
D. a budget hotel in the forest.

8. The various chores listed in lines 11–13 primarily serve as:

F. explanations of the minimal amount of work required to maintain the grounds.
G. examples illustrating the intense work the boys have to do to maintain the The Gables' trails.
H. illustrations of the competition between Jason and Paul.
J. specific details demonstrating how much harder Jason and Paul work than Mike.

9. Based on the passage's description of Mike, which of the following best characterizes his feelings about the summer as a whole?

A. He is fearful that he, Jason, and Paul will lose their jobs because of a lack of hard work at The Gables.
B. He is concerned that an incredible summer is coming to a tragic end.
C. He feels a sense of anticipatory nostalgia for the memorable summer, which distracts him from enjoying the moment.
D. He is happy that the summer is coming to an end.

10. In the context of the passage, the statement "...minimalist beauty was unfortunately also Paul's prison" (line 75–76) most nearly means that:

F. Paul perceives the simple beauty of the sea as restrictive.
G. Mike's appreciation of the landscape's beauty is more sophisticated than Paul's.
H. there are no elements in the simple landscape the boys could use to climb down or back up the cliff.
J. the boys see both beauty and darkness in the ocean landscape.

Passage II

SOCIAL SCIENCE: This passage is adapted from "Designing Cities: Forces of Democracy" by Ollie Sandoval. (©2017 by Society Press).

When it comes to designing the towns and cities in which we live, too often outcomes that affect entire communities, and indeed entire generations, are left to chance. Worse than chance. For in the absence of purposeful, democratic planning, the consequences of market forces are predictable: the market determines, with disinterest in human fulfillment, the shape of human space.

Perhaps the most striking view of what happens when development becomes untethered from democracy can be seen in the layout of post-World War II American suburbs, which developed largely without planning. With profit for developers and convenience for residents the only incentives at work, a massive sprawl discordant with fundamental human goals scarred the landscape. Major highways sped up commutes but created inescapable noise and impassable barriers that severed neighborhoods from one another; shopping plazas provided easy access to cheap goods but without thought for urban design or architecture, creating vast tracts of objectively ugly space regarded as the new "normal"; private homes provided massive square footage and private lawns but at the cost of the shared village space so vital to building the strong communities that had once defined the country.

The problem derives partly from the much-researched disconnect, indeed the contradiction, between immediate and delayed gratification, between spontaneous and planned decision-making. When given democratic choice (the right to vote in many societies, the choice of hypotheticals in research studies) people overwhelmingly choose community plans that prioritize quality of life over ease or profit: efficient public transportation over private cars and busy roads; walkable downtowns over retail sprawl; locally-owned businesses over chain superstores; public parks and preserved natural space over increased private space—in short, the very qualities that define the world's great communities, the sorts of places we would choose to visit.

And yet, in daily real-world decisions, when no such democratic choice is available, people routinely and directly contradict what they say they want. Homeowners purchase multiple cars and drive even when unnecessary, and the market reacts by calling for more and bigger roads. People seek out the absolute cheapest price for consumer products, without regard for the long-term effect such purchases, in the aggregate, will have on local business, wages, or quality of life. People choose private homes with large acreage, precluding the possibility of development that preserves natural, or any, public space. And as for the inadequate, unremarkable public space that is left, most of it preserved in small, unusable patches, the land falls into disuse, sending the market signal that less, not more, public land is desired. Thus the world in which we live, a result of many seemingly inconsequential decisions, comes to resemble the exact opposite of the world we say we want.

Here, it is important not to blithely cast blame. The fault lies not with the market itself, which has proved unsurpassed in its ability to efficiently generate and distribute wealth, nor with individuals, who after all are only rationally maximizing their own positions in the market as it exists. Instead, the blame lies in the failure of democratic systems to maintain the playing field on which markets and individuals interact. Markets are extraordinary economic engines but very poor engineers. Individuals are wise engineers, but, stripped of any reliable engineering projects, they resort reliably to impulsive, short-sighted choices. Democracies have long recognized these respective strengths and failings and so had, before the rise of the new market orthodoxy, reserved a central role for determining where and how the market operates, and where and how individuals make decisions, particularly in the planning of human space. The beautifully democratic result can be seen in counterexamples to the modern suburb—historic cities and towns with aspirational public art and architecture; central libraries; well-funded, well-used public parks; and thriving, walkable arts and business districts—which did not simply evolve from the small, cumulative decisions of individuals, but instead from democratic planning.

Unfortunately, at the local, state, and federal levels, governments have largely ceded their once-held power to the dispassionate hand of the market. Some—those absentee plaza developers, those free-market evangelists, those few triumphant commuters who have shaved ten minutes from a forty minute drive—have argued this is as it should be: democratic nations get what the market wants, and the market wants speed. It wants convenience. It wants profit for business and affordability for residents. But are these goals (and they are positive and valid goals) the exclusive claims of the market? Are they not democratic goals as well? More importantly, are they the only goals?

The market-centric argument, it seems, rests on a fundamental and historic civic error: America is not, nor has it ever been, a market society. No, America is, and has always been, a democratic society, one with a successful, high-functioning, regulated market economy. The distinction is crucial. For the power of democracy, the foundation upon which the country was originally built, means that the market is not destiny. Democracy, should towns and cities choose to take it back, would once again empower people to create the communities they want, not settle for the ones they merely get.

11. The main idea of the passage is that:

A. though they should be designed by democracy, cities are often accidents of market forces.
B. people prefer cities that are cheap and fast to those that are expensive and spread out.
C. American cities are designed by a democracy when they should be designed by a market.
D. post-World War II American suburbs are the model on which all of America should be designed.

12. The primary function of the fourth paragraph (lines 39–56) is to:

F. provide examples of American cities today.
G. explain the causes for a seemingly contradictory reality.
H. support an argument introduced in the third paragraph.
J. anticipate and refute a counterargument.

13. According to the passage, people choose communities that prioritize quality of life over ease and cost:

A. when they are making decisions in their daily lives.
B. when they are deciding spontaneously.
C. when they are given a choice in advance.
D. whenever they can.

14. The author's tone can best be described as:

F. concerned and emphatic.
G. enthusiastic and optimistic.
H. ambivalent and explanatory.
J. questioning and hopeful.

15. All of the following are results of post-World War II American suburbs EXCEPT:

A. convenience for residents.
B. shopping plazas.
C. profit for developers.
D. shared village space.

16. It can most reasonably be inferred that the author feels that modern suburbs are:

F. exquisite examples of democratic choice.
G. the result of unfortunate, spontaneous forces.
H. just as impressive as the world's most historic cities and towns.
J. desirable places to live.

17. The "free-market evangelists" (line 84) would argue that:

A. cities should prioritize minimizing costs for residents and maximizing financial gain for businesses.
B. locally-owned businesses should have priority over chain superstores.
C. art and architecture, central libraries, and parks are essential to a city.
D. the government should give more power to absentee plaza developers.

18. The passage makes use of all of the following literary devices EXCEPT:

F. rhetorical questions.
G. metaphor.
H. onomatopoeia.
J. personification

19. The word *ceded* (line 82) most nearly means:

A. kept.
B. maintained.
C. opposed.
D. abdicated.

20. Based on the passage, a society's markets create communities that:

F. lack elements that improve the population's quality of life, which exist when people are given time to make democratic decisions.
G. prioritize profit and convenience, benefiting both residents and developers more than any other prioritization could.
H. look exactly like those that citizens choose when given time to make a well-planned decision.
J. are undesirable places to live because they have no redeeming qualities.

Passage III

HUMANITIES: Passage A is adapted from the article "Dining and the Arts: a Delicate Balance" by Martina Arntz. (©2018 by Martina Arntz). Passage B is adapted from the article "The Pleasure of Cuisine" by Arthur MacNeil. (©2017 by Arthur MacNeil).

Passage A by Martina Arntz

The public's dismal view of fine dining has been made worse by social media. Scroll through Instagram, and the caricature–ready images abound: fussy arrangements of basic staples (asparagus teepees and Jackson Pollock abstractions of sauce); gamey, anachronistic meats (think organs, oxen); menus confusing detail for complexity (the shaved cheddar, Moroccan sea salt, California thyme, walnut crumble, and sorghum pasta is just mac n' cheese); portions measured for display, not for eating. The prices, crossing a social line from expensive to exclusionary, confirm the worst of the public's suspicions: the "art" of food is an indulgence for the idle elite.

And yet, the industry flourishes. Dedicated chefs continue to endure long hours and years of low pay to pursue the creation of fine food as a life's calling. Serious diners continue to pay sometimes exorbitant amounts for what they describe as the "sometimes-transcendent experience" of an extraordinary meal. And serious food writers continue to engage with food as art, convinced there is beauty, even depth, in sustenance. The sincere commitment of so many speaks to the existence of an art that is deeper than caricatures in glossy-looking photo feeds might suggest. Can the general public ever be convinced?

Some hope may lie in the writings of food critic Derek Silver, whose sensitivity to both the low and the high art of food may yet bridge the social divide. Silver uses his weekly food column to explore the culinary enclaves of his home city, Los Angeles, where he finds in its diverse street food scene not only authentic global cuisines—Mexican, Chilean, Korean, Japanese, Chinese, Filipino—but also a living food culture continuously mixing and inventing new experiences, both high and low. Silver knocks the charlatans who peddle overpriced "plate art," but remains open to the experience of seeing, smelling, tasting, feeling, and thinking about the depth and origin of extraordinary meals. Food, he argues, contains the roots of human culture. It can be an expression of human creativity as compelling as any found in the "traditional" arts—painting, sculpture, and the like.

Silver is particularly adept at challenging the critics of his thesis, who argue that food is a basic biological need, not an art. In response, Silver points out that all art operates with constraints, whether biological or market-based. The purity of film, for example, is constrained by the commercial demands of the film business. The purity of music is constrained by the biological human affinity for pattern and repetition. The truth is not that the culinary arts are any less "pure" than film, music, and literature, but rather that all arts are themselves less pure than many critics will admit. Purity, Silver suggests, is the real myth, and it's limiting the scope of artistic possibility.

Passage B by Arthur MacNeil

The problem with any consideration of food as art is the invariability of food's pleasures, which derive entirely from the hard-wired human drive for survival. Food should taste good and provide sustenance. Within those parameters, it's true there can be a fairly diverse expression of flavor and presentation. Just compare a dish of Pad Kee Mao to an English steak pie. But is the diversity of food analogous to the complexity of art? On the contrary, the biological necessity of food renders its claim on art—which through history has been chaotic, visionary, unpredictable, and challenging—impossible.

This isn't to say that food can't be compelling: it would be reductive to suggest that in food people seek only the fulfillment of primal drives. If that were the case, menus would consist only of the most indulgent combinations of fats, salts, and sugars, with carbohydrates, sodas, and nuggets of various shapes always assuming center stage. Superficial biological cravings would be curbed only by some vestigial biological intuition that one must eventually eat a vegetable, resulting in half-hearted gestures at salads and controlled portions, a kind of reversion to the mediocre mean (and a not-bad characterization of many fast food menus today).

However, human interest in food is demonstrably more complex than the vision marketed by fast food restaurants. Many menus are truly complex and daring, and the true diversity of individual tastes suggests there is more than mere biological craving at work when it comes to preparing and choosing food. As one example of just how psychological, and yes, creative, our interest in food can be, consider the unique human craving for spice. Where most species perceive spice as poison (as do most young and unexposed humans), cultural exposure leads many to find satisfaction in the pain of a spicy meal. With that kind of counterintuitive drive, who could argue that our interest in food derives merely from an interest in survival?

Yet to suggest that our diverse, complex taste in food is anything like our deep interest in the diversity or complexity of true art would be to draw a false equivalence. Where complexity in musical, narrative, and visual art is unconstrained, stemming from the vision of the artist, the chef has no choice but to create food that tastes, within broad but restrictive parameters, "good." The "art" of food is thus the art of popular appeal. True art can challenge and confront: the great stuff, even as it entertains, always does. But could one imagine the analogy of the challenging entree? The avant-garde steak, charred and difficult, but evocative of some historic pain? The post-modern carrots, roasted to challenge our conception of what a carrot even is? No, the defenders of the proposition that food is art are left defending an essentially untenable artistic position: that the "art," in order to satisfy a human need, must be palatable.

Questions 21–24 ask about Passage A.

21. According to Passage A, the street food scene in Los Angeles includes:

A. mostly expensive dishes considered fine cuisine.
B. work by popular fine dining chefs.
C. primarily foods originating in Europe.
D. traditional foods and new creations.

22. The main idea of the second paragraph (lines 13–23) is that the fine dining industry:

F. flourishes because most people believe in it.
G. has significantly lowered its prices over time.
H. is only enjoyed by food writers.
J. has its supporters, although the general public does not completely condone it.

23. In the context of Passage A, the author uses the lists in lines 3–10 in order to:

A. prove that social media is the key reason for fine dining's success.
B. illustrate the types of foods that the public criticizes.
C. celebrate the creations of famous chefs.
D. critique the elite customers of fine dining restaurants.

24. It can reasonably be inferred from Passage A that the critics of Derek Silver's work believe that:

F. food should reflect only its traditional origin.
G. there are multiple connections between food and the arts.
H. chefs should concentrate more on the presentation of their food.
J. food is not an art form.

Questions 25–27 ask about Passage B.

25. Passage B most nearly suggests that compared to animals and babies, adults think spices:

A. fulfill biological human needs.
B. could be used to diversify bland fast food menus.
C. can be a satisfying and interesting addition to food.
D. are dangerous to health and potentially poisonous.

26. In the context of Passage B, the author most likely uses the question in lines 98–99 to express the fact that food:

F. should be visually attractive in addition to appetizing.
G. is constrained by taste, while art can be more complex.
H. should mirror the trends of modern art.
J. can satisfy the body, even if it is not delicious.

27. In Passage B, the author includes the list of fats, salts, and sugars (line 67) in order to:

A. enumerate the ingredients that humans are naturally drawn to in foods.
B. provide examples of cravings that people ignore in favor of healthy choices.
C. prove that food can be just as complex as art.
D. appeal to the reader's interests by naming popular food groups.

Questions 28–30 ask about both passages.

28. Both David Silver's critics in Passage A and the author of Passage B would agree that:

F. food is more appealing if it is made in a creative way.
G. humans should eat food regardless of how it tastes.
H. food cannot be considered a true art.
J. the complexities of fine dining are completely worthless.

29. Which of the following statements best describes the difference in tone of the two passages?

A. Passage A is descriptive, whereas Passage B argues an opinion.
B. Passage A is critical, whereas Passage B is detached.
C. Passage A is satirical, whereas Passage B is optimistic.
D. Passage A is ironic, whereas Passage B is formal.

30. Compared to the author of Passage B, the author of Passage A provides more information about the:

F. human desires that drive interest in certain foods.
G. food culture in a particular location.
H. relationship between food and the arts.
J. public's cultural beliefs about food.

Passage IV

NATURAL SCIENCE: This passage is adapted from the article "Bomb Cyclone: Extreme Weather and Media Hysteria" by Aldin Van Houtem. (©2018 by Weather Founding Media).

In January 2018, a "bomb cyclone" dropped 13.6 inches of snow on New York City. Many New Yorkers were struck by the intensity of the language used to describe the storm, especially considering that, while certainly cause for a snow day, this snowstorm did not necessarily seem worthy of its hyperbolic name. But the title of "bomb cyclone" proved irresistible to media outlets chasing sensational headlines. Though The National Weather Service (NWS) simply warned followers that "heavy snow and ice" were expected, the vast majority of networks and newspapers seized upon the apocalyptic language—The Bomb Cyclone!—sensationalizing the event and bringing a misunderstood meteorological term into the common vernacular.

Meteorologists tried to inform the public that even though a "bomb cyclone" sounds extreme, the term has more to do with how the storm developed (which people do not experience on the ground) than with the storm's effects. The details are technical, precise, and wholly unsensational, but meteorologists hoped that educators might take advantage of the sensational headlines to introduce the public to the actual science behind how extreme weather patterns, including bomb cyclones, develop and evolve.

Extreme weather always occurs at what meteorologists call a weather front: the boundary between two air masses that differ in density, humidity, and temperature. When a region of warm air meets a region of cool air, barometric pressure drops drastically. As the air moves and begins to mix together, Earth's rotation creates the effect of a cyclone.

Generally speaking, cyclones are large air masses made of winds that spiral inward and rotate around a low-pressure center. The winds are guided by the subtropical jet stream—narrow, fast, twisting air currents that usher each cyclone through its two-to-six-day life cycle.

Cyclones are essential to the planet's general weather patterns. In fact, much of Earth's weather is driven by two varieties of cyclone: extratropical cyclones (also called mid-latitude cyclones or wave cyclones), which form in low-pressure areas, and anticyclones, which form in high-pressure areas. Extratropical cyclones cause rapid changes in temperature and can produce anything from cloudy days and rain showers to blizzards, tornadoes, and heavy gales. Anticyclones, in contrast, clear the skies and lead to cooler, drier weather. Meteorologists have researched these types of cyclones for years to understand their development and effects on broader weather patterns.

Meteorologists have developed two primary models for understanding cyclogenesis, the process that ultimately results in a cyclone. The Norwegian Cyclone Model, developed in World War I, was developed entirely from surface-based observations of weather. It posits that cyclones are created as they move along and up a frontal boundary of air. As a cold front overtakes a warm front, warm air is occluded—the process that takes place when the cold front of a rotating low-pressure system overtakes the warm front, forcing the warm air upward above a section of cold air—at the Earth's surface from the center of the cyclone, creating a cold environment.

The alternative model, the Shapiro-Keyser Model, was put forth by M.A. Shapiro and D. Keyser in an article published in the *Bulletin of the American Meteorological Society* in 1990. This model treats warm-type occlusions and warm fronts as equal, which means that cold fronts can travel perpendicularly across the warm front, as opposed to being occluded entirely. In addition to surface observations, the researchers used data from aircrafts that determined the vertical structure of northwest Atlantic fronts and helped to construct this model for oceanic cyclones. Meteorologists' understanding of these models has informed their present-day understanding—including the "bomb cyclone."

So what exactly is a "bomb cyclone"? What makes a storm a "bomb"? Decreasing atmospheric pressure is a characteristic of all storms, but so-called bombogenesis occurs when pressure drops at a particularly fast rate: at least 24 millibars in 24 hours.

On January 3, 2018, the extremely cold polar air that had chilled the East Coast of the United States since the holidays met the warm air that had descended over the ocean. In the Northern Hemisphere, this mixing occurs in a counterclockwise direction, which causes winds to blow from the northeast (a Nor'Easter). As the two mixed together, pressure fell quickly from Florida northward along the East Coast, resulting in bombogenesis and the subsequent January 4th winter storm.

This phenomenon is not rare—in fact, in October 2017, more than 80,000 buildings in Maine lost power after the remains of a tropical cyclone over the Atlantic met a Midwest cold front, causing strong winds to fell trees. A 2002 study found that there are about 45 bomb cyclones annually in the Northern Hemisphere.

Of course, the storm did end up bringing a significant amount of snowfall and far below average temperatures to the East Coast. It was important that people were conscious enough of the storm to plan for a snow day, so media outlets argued that using such extreme language ensured that people were aware of the extreme weather they would be encountering. Had they described it with its dictionary definition, would people have have been so attentive? We'll never know, but it will be incumbent upon media outlets in the future to be aware that ascribing such extremities to a rather common winter event can give cause for undue panic.

31. The overall organization of the passage is best described as:

A. an account of reactions to an event, followed by a scientific description of the phenomenon causing the event.
B. a chronological account of scientists' research on a particular bomb cyclone.
C. a series of historical examples that prove that bomb cyclones have existed for many centuries.
D. a collection of disproved theories about the genesis of bomb cyclones.

32. The main function of the tenth paragraph (lines 89–94) is to:

F. prove that a similar storm in Maine caused more severe consequences.
G. provide statistics about bomb cyclones in the Northern Hemisphere.
H. summarize the contributions of meteorologists who have studied cyclogenesis in the past.
J. provide examples that illustrate a common phenomenon.

33. Based on the information provided, one major difference between the Norwegian Cyclone and Shapiro-Keyser models is that the Shapiro-Keyser model:

A. was the original model developed by scientists studying cyclogenesis.
B. states that warm air is occluded by a cold front.
C. does not account for patterns from storms over the ocean.
D. included aircraft observations in addition to surface-based observation data.

34. The main idea of the last paragraph is that:

F. meteorologists are concerned about the dangerous effects of bomb cyclones.
G. cyclones are caused by a rapid drop in air pressure.
H. the naming of meteorological phenomena may have unintended consequences.
J. bomb cyclones cause an extreme amount of snow.

35. The passage makes clear all of the following EXCEPT:

A. bombogenesis occurs less often annually than do typical storms.
B. typical storms occur when pressure falls by at least 24 millibars in 24 hours.
C. bombogenesis does not necessarily cause a particularly severe snow storm, despite its intimidating name.
D. the Northern Hemisphere sees only about 45 bomb cyclones each year.

36. Based on the passage, the rotation direction of a Nor'Easter is the result of:

F. Earth's rotation and the cyclone's location in the Northern Hemisphere.
G. blizzards, tornadoes, and heavy gales.
H. its distinction as a bomb cyclone.
J. the time of year when the storm takes place.

37. The passage indicates that the media's use of the term "bomb cyclone" could potentially result in:

A. disagreement about the term's definition amongst meteorologists.
B. confusion with other extreme weather events such as mesocyclones and dust devils.
C. unnecessary alarm about a relatively common event.
D. amateur meteorologists and laypeople misunderstanding the science behind bombogenesis.

38. According to the passage, the life cycle of cyclones:

F. has not yet been determined by scientists.
G. is between two and six days.
H. takes place in January of each year.
J. depends on the particular type of cyclone.

39. It can reasonably be inferred from the passage that the author includes the public's reactions about the intensity of the term "bomb cyclone" (lines 2–6) primarily to:

A. introduce a discussion of the weather terminology.
B. explain the reasoning of meteorologists for naming storms.
C. highlight the intensity of the January 2018 storm in the Northeast.
D. illustrate the weather phenomena that are categorized as bomb cyclones.

40. As it is used in line 11, the phrase "seized upon" most nearly means:

F. snatched.
G. adopted.
H. grasped.
J. took control of.

Answer Key

Question	Answer	Tier	Main Idea	Specific Detail	Purpose
1.	D	2		--------	
2.	G	2	--------		
3.	C	2	--------		
4.	H	3			--------
5.	A	2		--------	
6.	J	1		--------	
7.	C	2		--------	
8.	F	1			--------
9.	C	2		--------	
10.	H	1		--------	
11.	A	2	--------		
12.	G	1			--------
13.	C	2		--------	
14.	F	2	--------		
15.	D	3		--------	
16.	G	2		--------	
17.	A	1		--------	
18.	H	3			--------
19.	D	1		--------	
20.	F	2		--------	
21.	D	2		--------	

Answer Key

Question	Answer	Tier	Main Idea	Specific Detail	Purpose
22.	J	1	________		
23.	B	1			________
24.	J	2		________	
25.	C	2		________	
26.	G	1			________
27.	A	1			________
28.	H	2	________		
29.	A	2	________		
30.	G	2		________	
31.	A	2	________		
32.	J	1			________
33.	D	2		________	
34.	H	1	________		
35.	B	3		________	
36.	F	2		________	
37.	C	2		________	
38.	G	2		________	
39.	A	1			________
40.	G	1		________	
Total	________		________	________	________

Congratulations on finishing the Chapter 4 Test! If you feel like you need more practice or guidance on any specific question type, work through or revisit the following pages:

- Main Idea - p. 51
- Specific Detail - p. 45
- Purpose - p. 53

Chapter 5

Practice Test 1

Congratulations on all the work you've done so far to better your ACT Reading score! In Chapters 5–7, you'll find three complete practice tests to work through, along with their answer keys.
In order to mimic an actual test day, you should:

- Find a quiet space to work with limited distractions
- Turn your cell phone off
- Set a timer for the correct amount of time
- Use a pencil rather than a pen
- Try out all of the great tactics you've learned from this book!

Answer keys and scoring rubrics can be found after each exam. If you find yourself having trouble with any particular question type, don't hesitate to read through those corresponding sections again. Learning to work through the ACT Reading section is a specific skill set that takes practice!

You can find scantron-style answer sheets at the end of this book that you can tear out if you'd like to replicate the full test-taking experience.

For Practice Test 1, flip to the next page!

READING TEST

35 Minutes — 40 Questions

DIRECTIONS: There are four passages in this test. Each passage is followed by several questions. Choose the best answer to each question and fill in the corresponding oval on your answer document. You may refer to the passages as often as necessary.

Passage I

LITERARY NARRATIVE: Passage A is adapted from the novel *Away and Up* by Fran Albertson. (©2018 by Storied). Passage B is adapted from the novel *Letting Go and Such* by Martina Masters. (©2017 by Storied).

Passage A by Fran Albertson

Christine sat on her dorm-standard XL twin bed and took a deep breath. After reinventing her entire wardrobe that fall, she was now left with the impossible task of strategically selecting and packing her entire new self for 5 three weeks with her family back home. Without their surveillance, the preppy gal clad in bright pastels had metamorphosed; she was a laid-back library dweller now, fitted in oversized sweaters and slouchy slacks. Itchy contacts had been ditched for a big pair of comfortable, won- 10 derfully un-fashionable glasses.

Would her parents complain? Or worse, worry? Would her mother express deep concern for her lost daughter's well-being? Christine's anxieties, many having nothing to do with her wardrobe, were nevertheless 15 imbuing all her clothes with horrible implications.

It was her first return home since she had begun college that September. With the independence of dorm life, no old habit or idea had been left unexamined. She had discovered, for instance, that she preferred morning cof- 20 fee to tea. Breakfast was better after class than before. Piles of clothing sat on the floor, since she did laundry only once a month—a far cry from what she and her high school friends had called the "Stafford Household Etiquette." On her own, she was the only Stafford present, 25 and her way reigned supreme.

She imagined the welcome home. Dad, with outstretched arms, would remark affectionately, "You grew! They must be feeding you fertilizer at that school!" Mother would begrudgingly laugh, annoyed that his pre- 30 dictable humor tickled her every time. Jimmy would run from his room, blabbering about his fifth grade orchestra recital and how she just has to watch the video and can we do it now and please let's do it right away. He had never lacked confidence, an admirable if somewhat ag- 35 gravating quality derived from their mother's inveterate optimism and slogans: "Hold your head up high," she'd say, and it was as though her brother would literally decide to raise his head and march about.

Still, Christine had taken a page or two out of that 40 book of fifth grade wisdom, spending less time worrying, more time simply being in her first semester. She had found a new self-confidence at school. How hard could it really be to carry that home? Well...hard. Christine's family, even in her imagination, mocked her new sense 45 of self. Behind the doors of her childhood home may be the most radical place she "held her head high" that year.

Passage B by Martina Masters

Of all the parents on the block, I was the only one who hadn't attended college. This fact had always made me feel like the runt of the litter—out of touch and not 50 up to snuff. I, of course, knew deep down that this one fact did not define me. Though I hadn't had traditional schooling, I still had a lot to be proud of, but it was easy to lose sight of my accomplishments when surrounded by others who had completed what I hadn't.

55 A product of the Summer of Love, I was raised in what some might call an unconventional household, where "Every day is an adventure," was my mother's guiding mantra. I woke to the sounds of our backyard roosters, the only feathered friends in our otherwise- 60 typical suburban neighborhood. After donning my fairy crown of flowers, I skipped to my backyard school where my parents taught me about whatever subject my quizzical mind could think up. I determined the curriculum, the schedule, the method of teaching. While such a system 65 did leave academic holes that I'd have to work to fill later in life, my curiosity helped me to learn the ins and outs of plants, my favorite subject.

Now the proud owner of a green thumb and a successful nursery, I wouldn't change my unusual school- 70 ing for the world. But with my children I've done things differently, or, in the eyes of everyone else, the same. I wanted their education to produce what my own did not: choice. The choice to attend college or start a business or travel the world. With education, I believe, comes oppor- 75 tunity, and I've sought to add structure to my own children's schooling.

And so it went that this fall, my oldest packed her bags and went off to college. Lauren's leaving for school was one of the proudest moments of my life, but I found 80 myself nervous for her return. She had experienced something I felt I had missed out on. Would she feel she had progressed beyond me, like she was returning, embarrassed, to some provincial past? The week before fall break, I wrung my hands in worry, nearly wearing down 85 the skin. That Friday, I stood on the porch as her car pulled in, counting down the seconds in my head.

Out of the car door walked a learned woman, confidently radiating her newfound sense of self. Inferiority was the last thing on my mind. I beamed with pride.

Questions 1–4 ask about Passage A.

1. The author mostly likely includes the details in lines 5–10 in order to:
   A. provide details about how Christine's clothing style has changed.
   B. indicate the disdain Christine's parents would feel about her clothing.
   C. argue that high schools should not require dress codes.
   D. suggest that Christine should take better care of her appearance.

2. It can most reasonably be inferred from Passage A that the independence Christine felt at college caused her to:
   F. appreciate her mother's rigid household rules.
   G. adapt to the habits of her fellow students.
   H. reexamine her habits and decide on new routines.
   J. care less about her own well-being.

3. The main idea of Passage A is that:
   A. out of all of her family members, Christine gets along best with her brother Jimmy.
   B. Christine has been enjoying her time away at college.
   C. Christine feels anxious about her return home from college.
   D. Christine's family did not want her to go away to college.

4. The quotation in lines 27–28 most nearly serves to:
   F. provide an example of why Christine feels anxious about her return home.
   G. emphasize the strict etiquette put in place by Christine's mother.
   H. illustrate the excitement Christine's father will feel when his daughter returns home.
   J. stress that Christine is not being properly fed at school.

Questions 5–7 ask about Passage B.

5. Which of the following questions is specifically answered in Passage B?
   A. What is the name of the school the narrator attended as a child?
   B. How many children does the narrator have?
   C. Why did Lauren decide to go to college?
   D. How is the narrator's education different from that of the other parents in the neighborhood?

6. The main idea of the second paragraph in Passage B (lines 55–67) is that:
   F. the narrator's parents put her at a severe academic disadvantage by homeschooling her.
   G. the narrator's atypical schooling allowed her to find a passion.
   H. gardening is the best career path for students who struggle in school.
   J. the narrator was directly affected by the time period in which she was born.

7. Which of the following best paraphrases the narrator's comments in lines 71–76?
   A. The narrator believes that all children should be required to attend school.
   B. According to the narrator, children should be able to choose how they want to be educated.
   C. A foundation in education would allow the narrator's children to choose their paths.
   D. The narrator hopes that her children will choose to become gardeners as adults.

Questions 8–10 ask about both passages.

8. Among the characters in both passages, which one is portrayed as being most confident?
   F. Lauren's mother in Passage B
   G. Jimmy in Passage A
   H. Christine in Passage A
   J. Christine's dad in Passage A

9. Compared to Passage B, Passage A provides more information regarding:
   A. a character's career choice.
   B. how a character has changed over time.
   C. the location of a character's college.
   D. the relationship between a mother and daughter.

10. Which of the following statements best captures a similarity between Christine in Passage A and the narrator of Passage B? Both characters:
    F. nervously anticipate a reunion with family members.
    G. have non-traditional views about education.
    H. feel anxious about returning to their childhood home.
    J. wonder about their relationship with their parents.

Passage II

SOCIAL SCIENCE: This passage is adapted from the article "Language Endangerment" by Thomas Frankle. (©2018 by Linguistical Quarterly).

When asked how many languages exist in the world today, many people, including those who live in large international cities, vastly underestimate the truth. Fifty? Five hundred? Some boldly guess a thousand. But the reality is, there are nearly seven thousand languages spoken across the world. The enormous margin of error in estimates is likely a consequence of the small number and big influence of just a handful of widely-spoken languages—and those same few languages dominate when it comes to usage in media and international business. Over a billion people, for example, speak Mandarin Chinese. Another billion-plus speak English. And Hindustani, Spanish, and Arabic each boast hundreds of millions of speakers worldwide. Put those numbers together, and nearly half of the world's population speaks one of only five major languages.

Given the cultural and economic dominance of the top five, it is perhaps understandable that most people are unaware of the thousands of other languages spoken in pockets throughout the world. Unfortunately, while easily explained, the lack of public awareness is contributing to an alarming global trend: language extinction. Of the roughly 7000 extant human languages—each a source of irreplaceable cultural knowledge—over two thousand are categorized as "endangered." What's worse, linguists estimate that by 2100, a majority of these endangered languages will no longer exist.

Language endangerment profoundly affects entire cultures, perhaps most directly by weakening a population's sense of identity, especially when cultural traditions—such as prayers, ceremonies—and greetings, rely on a disappearing language for true expression. While it's true that some traditions can survive the transition to a new language, many are inextricably connected to their original language context and are lost irretrievably when that language disappears.

A long history of colonization and a current trend toward globalism have accelerated language endangerment throughout the world. Of the 220 spoken languages in the United States alone, linguists have classified 140 as endangered. A typical case is Menominee, spoken by the Menominee people of northern Wisconsin. Fewer than 40 people are now Menominee speakers, and most are elderly. It is an all-too-common demographic shift that gravely endangers the future of any language.

Although some language endangerment is inevitable, governments, language communities, and organizations such as the United Nations Educational, Scientific, and Cultural Organization (UNESCO) are acting to prevent language loss. One important intervention has been to document language before it disappears. This includes recording language and its grammar through writing, dictionaries, audio, and video. Another proactive step has been to actively increase the number of speakers of endangered languages through education. Finally, language maintenance programs can offer support to endangered languages by promoting their use in education, communication, and culture. Linguists hope these efforts will be able to revitalize, or at least document for posterity, the endangered languages that still exist today.

Although the endangerment of a language is a sobering prospect, some cultures have successfully averted total language loss and have even revived their once-declining languages. The government of the Republic of Ireland has taken steps to increase the number of Irish speakers (which, as of 2016, was about 75,000 daily speakers). In order to ensure the future cultural and political relevance of Irish, the Irish constitution lists it as the first official language of the republic and requires the names of places on maps and road signs to be written in Irish. The federal government of Ireland has also made Irish a required subject in public education from primary through secondary schools. The Irish language remains alive through the media, where Irish-language programs are produced for radio and television. Similarly, Irish literature remains a thriving art. Similar programs have been successful in New Zealand, which has staged a successful revitalization of the Māori language by teaching Māori in "language nests," preschools for children aged 0–4. Māori is also now taught in bilingual and immersion programs in schools.

Language endangerment, while still not an area of concern in the mainstream, has become a central focus of linguists and anthropologists determined to protect the irreplaceable history that the world's languages not only preserve but continue to foster. Without the successful efforts of these determined researchers, the cultural traditions embedded in endangered languages will remain in jeopardy.

11. One main idea of the passage is that endangered languages:

A. can all be saved if governments, language communities, and organizations implement intervention efforts.
B. make up over half of all spoken languages today.
C. impact a culture's identity and ability to preserve history and tradition.
D. create a well-known problem that all societies around the world are actively working to correct.

12. Which of the following questions is NOT directly answered by the passage?

F. How many languages have become extinct over time?
G. How many languages are spoken across the world today?
H. What are the five most common languages in the world?
J. How many languages in the world are categorized as endangered?

13. The author most likely includes the sixth paragraph (lines 61–81) in order to:

A. provide examples of successful language revitalization programs.
B. dispute the claim that many languages are endangered today.
C. detail the prevalence of the Irish language throughout Europe.
D. emphasize the important role the Republic of Ireland has played in preserving languages worldwide.

14. The passage indicates that language revitalization programs are:

F. unfortunately always hopeless.
G. potentially successful efforts to save endangered languages.
H. international collaborations requiring the cooperation of many individuals.
J. successful only in countries like Ireland.

15. It can most likely be inferred from the passage that the Menominee language:

A. is currently being documented in a preservation program run by the community's elderly.
B. was at one time endangered but has been successfully revived.
C. became extinct years ago.
D. is still endangered today.

16. The author most likely includes quotation marks around the phrase "language nests" (line 79) in order to:

F. credit a New Zealand government official with the invention of a new phrase.
G. set aside a specialized term that readers may not know the definition of.
H. directly quote a Māori speaker.
J. emphasize a sarcastic remark regarding the Māori language.

17. The passage most strongly implies that people's estimates of the number of languages in the world are:

A. most accurate when the person guessing lives in a large international city.
B. correct in assuming that there are about five hundred spoken languages in the world.
C. incorrect because the frequent death of endangered languages means that the number is constantly changing.
D. often hugely underestimated due to the prevalence of the most popular languages.

18. According to the passage, language maintenance can occur through all of the following EXCEPT:

F. audio recording.
G. colonization.
H. education programs.
J. literature.

19. As it is used in lines 34–35, the phrase "inextricably connected to" most nearly means:

A. in no way related to.
B. hopelessly tangled with.
C. incapable of being separated from.
D. unable to understand how it is linked to.

20. In the passage, all of the following are examples of languages that are currently or were, at one point, endangered EXCEPT:

F. Menominee.
G. Māori.
H. Hindustani.
J. Irish.

Passage III

HUMANITIES: This passage is adapted from the article "A Push for Exploration" by Cadance Willhout. (©2016 by Anthro Up).

Lacking the clear utilitarian purpose too often demanded of science, the field of exploration now occupies an underfunded niche, one dominated by magazines and television shows that sell exotic photographs and footage of strange and beautiful places. It's a vital niche to be sure, one that promotes the aesthetic wonders of our planet, but a niche nonetheless, often politically and economically marginalized. The problem of underfunding is particularly severe in the field of deep sea exploration.

In the United States, for example, funding for deep sea exploration is dwarfed by funding for nearly all other government-funded scientific endeavors. Compare the National Aeronautics and Space Administration's 3.5 billion dollar budget (NASA projects have clear commercial, military, and political application) to the National Oceanic and Atmospheric Administration's paltry 25 million. Extreme as the disparity may seem, many educated policymakers claim that ocean exploration simply does not stand up to the cost/benefit analysis that determines all scientific funding. From a utilitarian point of view, their perspective is sound. But science has never been, and will suffer if it comes to be, strictly utilitarian. There must be an insistence that great science has always been motivated not only by logic but also by those deep feelings of wonder and astonishment we have unfortunately considered incidental. If undersea exploration is to be embraced, we must do away with the false dichotomy that has separated science from art.

Today, when it comes to policy decisions, that sense of wonder is being written off and replaced by a sense of utilitarianism. Once a novel contribution to dinner party trivia, the now-commonplace statistic that 70% of the world's oceans remain unexplored has become pop-cultural cliché. More concerningly, the sense of wonder the statistic once inspired—how is it possible to have seen so little of our own planet? What might our unknown world contain?—has today given way to blithe resignation, the kind that so often derives from easy, trivial knowledge. The ocean, some people now explain, is simply too deep. Forty-five million feet of water pressure would crush any human-made object.

The casual acceptance of this enormous blank smudge on our world map is a strange anomaly in the history of a sea-faring species, one known to enter, often at unthinkable cost, every square inch of its planet. We are the species that, thousands of years ago, without compass or map, took wooden canoes to the horizon of the Pacific Ocean. The species that traveled thousands of miles in open water to discover the islands—needles in a haystack—of Polynesia. It's true that exploration has, at times, been prompted by necessity, but more often it has been inspired and sustained by little more (or less) than our instinctive drive to see what has never been seen before. From this perspective, political disinterest in exploring our own planet's seas seems due to a failure to embrace the vital role that imagination plays in science.

Picture for a moment the world beneath the waves. Most of us will conjure a haze of sediment, a whir of salt and sand, an impenetrable expanse, mostly darkness. If visible at all, the seafloor in the human imagination is a denuded plain, all sand and rock (ironically, the closest visual analogy is a desert) punctuated intermittently, perhaps, by the oasis of a reef. For some, this image evokes a deep fear of the infinite, for others a minimalist beauty. The problem is neither fear nor aesthetic appreciation will lead us into the unknown. Because both our primal fear and our appreciation of minimalist beauty drive us to retreat from complexity and mystery. What the science of deep sea exploration needs, if it is to recapture the public's interest, is a revival of that sense of possibility that accompanied our first entry into the water as a species. A reawakening of stories, of myth, of belief in a life and a world beyond our own.

One such place we might reawaken the mystery that inspires exploration is in museums. In a nondescript tank in the basement of the London Museum, one of the only complete specimens of a giant squid lies suspended in a small sea of formaldehyde. Her body is twenty-eight feet long, prostrate, tentacles held in supplication. Visitors can visit, walk around the tank, and peer into the glass at a real-life mystery. Scientists know little about her origin or her history, only that she was briefly alive near the surface of the ocean off the coast of the Falkland Islands. The giant squid is rarely observed, never in its deepest habitat where it hunts and sleeps at depths humans have never explored. But to look into her eye is to look, undeniably, into evidence of a convergently-evolved intelligence that is broad, deep, and totally separate from our own. She reminds us that the ocean is worth exploring not for any prospect of wealth or access to natural resources, but simply because it is a world beyond our own. And that exploration itself may be a forgotten form of art.

21. Which of the following statements best captures the general theme of the passage?

A. Space exploration has more immediate importance than ocean exploration.
B. Scientists should capture more specimens like the giant squid in the London Museum.
C. Government program budgets should be determined pragmatically.
D. The importance of exploring the oceans should not be overlooked.

22. It can most reasonably be inferred from the statement in lines 17–20 that the logic against exploration includes:

F. people's enthusiasm for deep sea exploration.
G. society's distaste for underwater creatures.
H. more pressing social and economic concerns.
J. the triviality of information about the oceans.

23. The primary function of the fourth paragraph (lines 42–56) is to:

A. explain why humans chose to explore the Pacific Ocean.
B. contrast humans' current drive to explore with that of the past.
C. prove that politics is detrimental to human exploration of the seas.
D. provide background information about deep sea exploration.

24. According to the passage, an aspect of the deep sea that may prohibit exploration is the:

F. unknown species that reside in the depths.
G. water pressure that can crush a human-made object.
H. unappealing appearance of the seafloor.
J. limited quantity of oxygen under the water.

25. As it is used in line 27, the word *embraced* most nearly means:

A. forced.
B. supported.
C. encircled.
D. grasped.

26. According to the passage, the giant squid specimen in the London Museum:

F. spent its entire life in shallow waters near the coast of the Falkland Islands.
G. is only accessible to scientists who want to further study the species.
H. is closely related to many of the other similar squid specimens at other museums.
J. occupied a habitat deeper in the ocean than humans have explored.

27. The author indicates that most people imagine the seafloor to be:

A. a desert-like plain void of living things.
B. similar to images of the Milky Way in space.
C. a location that would be easy to explore.
D. full of strange creatures like giant squid.

28. "The unknown" mentioned in line 66 most nearly refers to:

F. the unexplored deep sea.
G. desert landscapes.
H. deep fear of the infinite.
J. a haze of sediment.

29. In the passage, the author mentions all of the following as reasons why humans have not further explored the deep ocean EXCEPT:

A. ocean travel has been unsuccessful for thousands of years.
B. policymakers cannot justify the funding.
C. the water pressure is so great that human-made objects would be crushed.
D. people assume it is too challenging and, as a result, impossible.

30. Based on the passage, which of the following best describes the author's opinion of deep sea exploration? The author:

F. thinks that people should focus on the practical concerns of oceanic exploration.
G. prefers space exploration to deep sea exploration.
H. believes that exploration should be motivated by both logic and curiosity.
J. hopes to see the results of deep sea exploration but considers it impossible.

Passage IV

NATURAL SCIENCE: This passage is adapted from the article "Unearthing the Thylacine" by Jim Luciano. (©2017 by BioEngineering Monthly).

At first glance, the thylacine, also known as the Tasmanian tiger, may seem like an unlikely candidate for current cutting-edge scientific research: the species, after all, has been officially extinct since 1936. Yet, researchers believe a recently-discovered treasure trove of genetic material from this dog-like marsupial may hold important clues about evolutionary processes, particularly the process of convergent evolution. Using preserved DNA from the thylacine's pouch young—joeys younger than four months old—scientists hope to decipher the thylacine's genetic code, and with it, important clues about how changes in DNA may lead to changes in a species' environmental adaptations.

Even when thylacine were alive, humans exhibited remarkably little curiosity (and knew remarkably little) about the species. At the height of its reign over 3,000 years ago, the thylacine lived in a relatively sparsely-populated Oceania, a region spanning Melanesia, Micronesia, Polynesia, and Australasia. By the time European settlers arrived on the Australian continent, the native thylacine population had already dwindled. Those thylacine that remained unfortunately came into immediate conflict with the new human shepherds, who, from the perspective of the thylacine, had arrived with a surplus of docile food. Farmers offered hunting bounties to protect their herds, a strategy that proved all too effective at eradicating the strange striped native "dog" many considered to be nothing but a threat. Wiped out from the mainland entirely, the thylacine managed to survive only as a small population off the coast of Australia, on the island of Tasmania. There, the isolated thylacines suffered from a lack of genetic diversity, leading to poor health and increased susceptibility to disease. In 1936, the last known thylacine died in captivity at the island's Hobart Zoo. Biologists believe that human intervention ultimately caused the thylacine's extinction.

So why the sudden scientific interest in a relatively obscure, extinct animal that attracted little interest even in life? To put it simply: convergent evolution. Convergent evolution is the development of similar traits in animals not closely related by genetics, but adapted in similar ways to the environment. The thylacine offers one of history's great convergent evolutionary cases, which can be seen physically in its strange hybrid appearance: striped like a tiger, but with body and head strongly resembling those of the canids (dingos, wolves, and even domesticated dogs).

In fact, the striking visual resemblance between canids and the thylacine is one of the most compelling cases of convergent evolution ever observed: the two species diverged 160 million years ago. By studying the species' relationship to one another, researchers seek to learn how two genetically dissimilar animals adapted to similar environments, and whether or not those similarities in phenotype are reflected by similarities in genotype.

The fact is, the exact mechanisms of convergent evolution remain elusive, with our current understanding based only on a few studies. To date, one of the most important studies took place in the 1960s, when scientists discovered two convergent species of fish that had been separated by the vast ocean between the Arctic and the Antarctic. First, in the Antarctic, scientists discovered a fish with characteristics that helped it survive the frigid waters. This fish species had evolved glycoproteins circulating in its blood, which performed the same function that antifreeze does in an automobile, lowering the temperature at which the fish's bodily fluids freeze and surrounding tiny ice crystals to prevent the ice from spreading. The same remarkable adaptation was then found in Arctic fish—very different waters, very different gene pool. The study has been foundational to the theory that, given similar environments, wildly different genomes often result in strikingly similar adaptations.

Other anecdotal cases of convergent evolution, however, have yielded results that lead to contradictory theories, suggesting that convergent evolution will usually be reflected in DNA. And therein lies the urgency within the scientific community to fully map the genome of the thylacine. Biologists currently believe that the most overt shared characteristics between the thylacine and the canids—including similarly shaped teeth and skulls—likely resulted from similar environmental needs, namely the species' similarly carnivorous diets. The question is, will researchers find that, as with the Arctic and Antarctic fish, the physical similarities do not result from genetic similarities? The recovered DNA of the thylacine offers a unique opportunity to more fully understand a species thought to have been completely lost to the world, and to further grapple with the mysteries of convergent evolution.

31. The main purpose of this passage is to:

A. discuss scientific innovations that will eventually lead to de-extinction technologies.
B. examine the physical similarities and differences between domesticated dogs and thylacines.
C. highlight specific methodologies that will further the theory of convergent evolution.
D. describe possible scientific discoveries that may result from recently discovered genetic material.

32. The purpose of the fifth paragraph (lines 57–74) is most likely to:

F. illustrate the importance of a discovery with an analogous example.
G. contrast convergent evolution involving two fish species with convergent evolution between the thylacine and domesticated dog.
H. explain how physical similarities often result from the same genetic evolution.
J. define the concept of convergent evolution.

33. According to the passage, what would scientists expect of the thylacine and domesticated dog based on previous conclusions regarding Arctic and Antarctic fish?

A. Physical similarities between the two would not necessarily correlate with genetic similarities.
B. Physical similarities between the two would likely correlate with genetic similarities.
C. Characteristics shared between the two could be traced back to a common ancestor.
D. Differences between the two would be purely coincidental.

34. The passage suggests that convergent evolution usually occurs in animals that:

F. are genetically similar.
G. express similar traits and are located extremely far from one another.
H. engage in similar lifestyles but do not share a common ancestor.
J. live in close proximity and learn similar behaviors from one another.

35. The main idea of the third paragraph (lines 37–47) is that:

A. scientists must use a particular methodology to study an extinct species.
B. extinct species can be studied to learn more about convergent evolution.
C. dog-like animals are most likely to demostrate convergent evolution.
D. the thylacine and canid species represent the most important case of convergent evolution.

36. The passage indicates that compared to canids, the thylacine has:

F. a carnivorous appetite dictated by habitat.
G. an identical evolutionary ancestry.
H. a similar diet, likely resulting in similar physical characteristics.
J. a dissimilar diet yet similar physical characteristics.

37. As it is used in line 25, the word *bounties* most nearly means:

A. large amounts.
B. wide varieties.
C. trade agreements.
D. financial incentives.

38. The passage indicates that the main cause for the extinction of the thylacine was:

F. increased susceptibility to disease.
G. human interference.
H. declining genetic diversity.
J. poor health.

39. It can be reasonably inferred that the phrase "remarkable adaptation" (line 70) refers to:

A. ice crystals within the Arctic and Antarctic.
B. intense blood circulation.
C. the presence of antifreeze within the bloodstream of the fish.
D. the presence of proteins that regulate temperature within the bloodstream of the fish.

40. The passage makes clear which of the following about the discovery of preserved thylacine pouch young?

F. Preserved DNA may allow scientists to study the species' genetic code.
G. The discovery will help scientists find a better environment for the thylacine.
H. Scientists would have preferred to study a fully-grown animal.
J. Pouch young can be compared to newborn canids.

STOP: END OF TEST 1

5.1 Answer Key

<table>
<tr><th>Question Number</th><th>Correct Answer</th><th>Question Type</th><th>Question Tier</th></tr>
<tr><td colspan="4">LITERARY NARRATIVE</td></tr>
<tr><td>1</td><td>A</td><td>Purpose</td><td>1</td></tr>
<tr><td colspan="4">A. In lines 5–10, “metamorphosed” indicates change and “oversized sweaters and slouchy slacks” has a positive tone.
B. The noun “Christine’s parents” is not mentioned.
C. The purpose of the sentence is not to argue about high school dress codes.
D. The sentence has a positive tone about Christine’s clothing.</td></tr>
<tr><td>2</td><td>H</td><td>Specific Detail</td><td>2</td></tr>
<tr><td colspan="4">Lines 17–18 show that no habits were left unexamined.</td></tr>
<tr><td>3</td><td>C</td><td>Main Idea</td><td>2</td></tr>
<tr><td colspan="4">A. Jimmy is mentioned only once in the passage.
B. Christine’s return home for break is the focus of the passage overall.
C. Christine worries about her family mocking her and thinks it will be hard to have self-confidence.
D. The passage does not mention Christine’s family not wanting her to go to college.</td></tr>
<tr><td>4</td><td>H</td><td>Purpose</td><td>1</td></tr>
<tr><td colspan="4">F. Dad is “affectionate” towards Christine.
G. Christine’s mother is not the one speaking in this quotation.
H. Dad has “outstretched arms.”
J. Although the words “feeding you fertilizer” are included, this is not a literal statement.</td></tr>
<tr><td>5</td><td>D</td><td>Specific Detail</td><td>2</td></tr>
<tr><td colspan="4">Lines 47–48 say that the narrator “was the only one who hadn’t attended college.”</td></tr>
<tr><td>6</td><td>G</td><td>Main Idea</td><td>1</td></tr>
<tr><td colspan="4">F. The tone of the paragraph is positive, which does not match with a severe disadvantage.
G. Reread the first and last sentence. The narrator had an “unconventional” childhood which allowed her to fulfill her “curiosity” for plants.
H. The narrator indicates that gardening was a great career path for her but does not make a blanket statement that it’s best for all struggling students.
J. The time frame of the “Summer of Love” is a detail mentioned only once, not a main idea.</td></tr>
<tr><td>7</td><td>C</td><td>Specific Detail</td><td>1</td></tr>
<tr><td colspan="4">In lines 71–73, the narrator states that she wants her children’s education to produce “choice.”</td></tr>
<tr><td>8</td><td>G</td><td>Specific Detail</td><td>2</td></tr>
<tr><td colspan="4">In paragraph 4 of Passage A, the passage states that Jimmy “had never lacked confidence.”</td></tr>
<tr><td>9</td><td>B</td><td>Specific Detail</td><td>2</td></tr>
<tr><td colspan="4">The last paragraph of passage A repeats the word “radical,” referring to a radical change.</td></tr>
<tr><td>10</td><td>F</td><td>Main Idea</td><td>2</td></tr>
<tr><td colspan="4">F. Passage A uses words like “anxieties” and “mocked”; Passage B uses the words “nervous” and “inferiority.”
G. Passage A does not mention Christine’s views of education.
H. The narrator of Passage B is not returning to her childhood home.
J. The narrator of Passage B does not analyze her relationship with her parents.</td></tr>
</table>

<table>
<tr><th>Question Number</th><th>Correct Answer</th><th>Question Type</th><th>Question Tier</th></tr>
<tr><td colspan="4">SOCIAL SCIENCE</td></tr>
<tr><td>11</td><td>C</td><td>Main Idea</td><td>2</td></tr>
<tr><td colspan="4">A. The passage includes details about intervention efforts, but as a detail, not the main idea.
B. The passage states that 2000 of 7000 human languages are considered endangered.
C. The last paragraph summarizes the main idea: language endangerment must be addressed, or "the cultural traditions embedded in endangered languages will remain in jeopardy."
D. The last paragraph states that language endangerment is "not an area of concern in the mainstream."</td></tr>
<tr><td>12</td><td>F</td><td>Specific Detail</td><td>3</td></tr>
<tr><td colspan="4">F. No details in the passage state precisely how many languages have been endangered over time.
G. Paragraph 2 states that 7000 languages are spoken across the world.
H. Paragraph 1 lists Mandarin, English, Hindustani, Spanish, and Arabic as the five major languages.
J. Paragraph 2 states that 2000 languages are currently categorized as endangered.</td></tr>
<tr><td>13</td><td>A</td><td>Purpose</td><td>1</td></tr>
<tr><td colspan="4">A. In the sixth paragraph, Ireland represents an example supporting the claim that "some cultures have successfully averted total language loss."
B. The paragraph does not "dispute" any claim that language is endangered.
C. The paragraph does not mention the use of Irish outside of Ireland.
D. The paragraph focuses on preserving language in Ireland, not worldwide.</td></tr>
<tr><td>14</td><td>G</td><td>Specific Detail</td><td>2</td></tr>
<tr><td colspan="4">Paragraph 6 and the conclusion suggest that language revitalization efforts have already had some success.</td></tr>
<tr><td>15</td><td>D</td><td>Specific Detail</td><td>2</td></tr>
<tr><td colspan="4">Paragraph 4 uses Menominee as an example of an endangered language.</td></tr>
<tr><td>16</td><td>G</td><td>Purpose</td><td>1</td></tr>
<tr><td colspan="4">F. The paragraph does not attribute the phrase "language nest" to a government official.
G. The quotation marks signal that the phrase "language nest" is being used to refer to schools.
H. No specific Māori speaker is mentioned.
J. The tone of the paragraph is not sarcastic.</td></tr>
<tr><td>17</td><td>D</td><td>Specific Detail</td><td>2</td></tr>
<tr><td colspan="4">Lines 6–9 state that people probably underestimate the total number of languages as "a consequence of the small number and big influence of just a handful of widely-spoken languages..."</td></tr>
<tr><td>18</td><td>G</td><td>Specific Detail</td><td>3</td></tr>
<tr><td colspan="4">F. Paragraph 5 states that interventions include "writing, dictionaries, audio, and video."
G. Lines 37–39 mention colonization as a factor accelerating language endangerment.
H. Paragraph 5 states that "proactive step has been to actively increase the number of speakers of endangered languages through education."
J. Lines 75–76 indicate that "Irish literature remains a thriving art."</td></tr>
<tr><td>19</td><td>C</td><td>Specific Detail</td><td>1</td></tr>
<tr><td colspan="4">Lines 28–29 state that "language endangerment profoundly affects entire cultures," indicating that culture cannot be separated from language.</td></tr>
</table>

<table>
<tr><th>Question Number</th><th>Correct Answer</th><th>Question Type</th><th>Question Tier</th></tr>
<tr><td>20</td><td>H</td><td>Specific Detail</td><td>3</td></tr>
<tr><td colspan="4">F. Paragraph 4 discusses Menominee.
G. Paragraph 6 discusses Māori.
H. Hindustani is mentioned in Paragraph 1 as an example of a major spoken language.
J. Paragraph 6 discusses Irish.</td></tr>
<tr><td colspan="4">HUMANITIES</td></tr>
<tr><td>21</td><td>D</td><td>Main Idea</td><td>2</td></tr>
<tr><td colspan="4">A. Space exploration is not a main theme. While space exploration has a bigger budget, that doesn’t necessarily make it more important.
B. The giant squid is not a main theme. While the giant squid is an example of the wonder of the deep ocean, the passage doesn’t state that more should be captured.
C. Government programs are not a main theme. In contrast, the author actually argues for science motivated by curiosity, not just practicality.
D. Throughout the passage, the author advocates for the importance of deep sea exploration, despite the challenges it presents.</td></tr>
<tr><td>22</td><td>H</td><td>Specific Detail</td><td>1</td></tr>
<tr><td colspan="4">According to lines 17–20, “many educated policymakers claim that ocean exploration simply does not stand up to the cost/benefit analysis that determines all scientific funding.” Exploration is, therefore, a less pressing concern.</td></tr>
<tr><td>23</td><td>B</td><td>Purpose</td><td>1</td></tr>
<tr><td colspan="4">A. Human exploration of the Pacific Ocean doesn’t explain why this paragraph is relevant to the passage.
B. Humans used to be motivated to explore, but they aren’t anymore. The author uses the past as evidence to support his argument that sea exploration should once again become a priority.
C. There is no “proof” in the passage that politics have hurt sea exploration.
D. The paragraph details history about exploring ocean surfaces and islands, not underwater.</td></tr>
<tr><td>24</td><td>G</td><td>Specific Detail</td><td>2</td></tr>
<tr><td colspan="4">Lines 40–41 state, “Forty-five million feet of water pressure would crush any human-made object.”</td></tr>
<tr><td>25</td><td>B</td><td>Specific Detail</td><td>1</td></tr>
<tr><td colspan="4">Lines 22–28 discuss the “deep feelings of wonder and astonishment” related to undersea exploration. The tone of this sentence indicates that undersea exploration should be supported.</td></tr>
<tr><td>26</td><td>J</td><td>Specific Detail</td><td>2</td></tr>
<tr><td colspan="4">According to lines 84–86, the squid normally lives “at depths humans have never explored.”</td></tr>
<tr><td>27</td><td>A</td><td>Specific Detail</td><td>2</td></tr>
<tr><td colspan="4">The fourth paragraph details “the world beneath the waves,” describing it as “dark,” “denuded,” and with the “closest visual analogy” to a desert. A is the only answer that fits the description provided.</td></tr>
<tr><td>28</td><td>F</td><td>Specific Detail</td><td>1</td></tr>
<tr><td colspan="4">This paragraph is talking about “the world beneath the waves” that people have to imagine because they don’t know what it actually looks like.</td></tr>
<tr><td>29</td><td>A</td><td>Specific Detail</td><td>3</td></tr>
<tr><td colspan="4">A. This detail is not mentioned in the passage.
B. Lines 17–20 state that ocean exploration “does not stand up to the cost/benefit analysis.”
C. Lines 40–41 state, “Forty-five million feet of water pressure would crush any human-made object.”
D. Lines 29–40 state, “the sense of wonder...has given way to resignation...the ocean is simply too deep.”</td></tr>
</table>

<table>
<tr><th>Question Number</th><th>Correct Answer</th><th>Question Type</th><th>Question Tier</th></tr>
<tr><td>30</td><td>H</td><td>Main Idea</td><td>2</td></tr>
<tr><td colspan="4">F. In contrast, the author argues for exploration motivated by curiosity, not just necessity.
G. While the author mentions NASA's very high space exploration budget, it is simply to argue that sea exploration deserves more funding.
H. Lines 22–26: "There must be an insistence that great science has always been motivated not only by logic, but also by those deep feelings of wonder and astonishment..."
J. While the author doesn't have solutions for some of the challenges presented, he still argues that "casual acceptance" of impossibility is not acceptable.</td></tr>
<tr><td colspan="4">NATURAL SCIENCE</td></tr>
<tr><td>31</td><td>D</td><td>Purpose</td><td>2</td></tr>
<tr><td colspan="4">A. De-extinction technologies are not a detail mentioned in the passage.
B. The similarities between canids and the thylacine are an important detail but still support a bigger main idea.
C. The passage doesn't give any details about the "specific methodologies."
D. Reread the intro and conclusion paragraphs. The passage provides an overview of possible scientific discoveries related to convergent evolution.</td></tr>
<tr><td>32</td><td>F</td><td>Purpose</td><td>1</td></tr>
<tr><td colspan="4">F. The paragraph uses the analogous example of the Arctic and Antarctic fish to illustrate the significance of studying species that exhibit convergent evolution.
G. The paragraph primarily compares the convergent evolution of two fish species to the convergent evolution of thylacine and canids. It does not contrast the examples.
H. The paragraph does not "explain" how anything happens. It simply describes it.
J. The paragraph does not "define" any concepts. Primarily, it illustrates a concept.</td></tr>
<tr><td>33</td><td>A</td><td>Specific Detail</td><td>2</td></tr>
<tr><td colspan="4">Lines 85–87 state, "will researchers find that, as with the Arctic and Antarctic fish, the physical similarities do not result from genetic similarities?"</td></tr>
<tr><td>34</td><td>H</td><td>Specific Detail</td><td>2</td></tr>
<tr><td colspan="4">The passage mentions the similar lifestyles of the thylacine and canids, as well as the similar lifestyles of two convergently-evolved fish species.</td></tr>
<tr><td>35</td><td>B</td><td>Main Idea</td><td>1</td></tr>
<tr><td colspan="4">A. The paragraph does not discuss the methodology scientists will use.
B. The paragraph mentions the concept of convergent evolution and provides the thylacine as an example.
C. This is a detail and is not based on the information in the paragraph.
D. While the thylacine is a given example, it is not said to be the most important case.</td></tr>
<tr><td>36</td><td>H</td><td>Specific Detail</td><td>2</td></tr>
<tr><td colspan="4">Lines 80–84 state, "Biologists currently believe that the... similarly shaped teeth and skulls...likely resulted from... the species' similarly carnivorous diets."</td></tr>
<tr><td>37</td><td>D</td><td>Specific Detail</td><td>1</td></tr>
<tr><td colspan="4">According to lines 25–28, farmers offered payments, or "bounties" to encourage the hunting of the thylacine.</td></tr>
<tr><td>38</td><td>G</td><td>Specific Detail</td><td>2</td></tr>
<tr><td colspan="4">Lines 35–36 state, "Biologists believe that human intervention ultimately caused the thylacine's extinction."</td></tr>
</table>

<table>
<tr><th>Question Number</th><th>Correct Answer</th><th>Question Type</th><th>Question Tier</th></tr>
<tr><td>39</td><td>D</td><td>Specific Detail</td><td>1</td></tr>
<tr><td colspan="4">Lines 65–70 state, “This fish species had evolved glycoproteins circulating in its blood, which performed the same function that antifreeze does in an automobile...lowering the temperature at which the fish’s bodily fluids freeze...”</td></tr>
<tr><td>40</td><td>F</td><td>Specific Detail</td><td>2</td></tr>
<tr><td colspan="4">The first paragraph states that “Using preserved DNA from the thylacine’s pouch young...scientists hope to decipher the thylacine’s genetic code.”</td></tr>
</table>

Raw Score: ___ / 40

Converted Score: ___ / 36

5.2 Scoring Rubric

Score Conversion[1]

Scaled Score	Raw Score	Raw Score	Scaled Score
1	0	19	**19**
2	–	20–21	**20**
3	1	22	**21**
4	2	23–24	**22**
5	–	25	**23**
6	3	26	**24**
7	–	27	**25**
8	4	28	**26**
9	5	29	**27**
10	6	30	**28**
11	7	31	**29**
12	8–9	32	**30**
13	10–11	33	**31**
14	12	34–35	**32**
15	13–14	36	**33**
16	15	37	**34**
17	16	38	**35**
18	17–18	39–40	**36**

[1]Score Conversions are general estimates based on the average correlations between raw scores and scaled scores as seen on recent ACT exams. They are meant to be used as such: general estimates.

Chapter 6

Practice Test 2

Remember to...

- Find a quiet space to work with limited distractions
- Turn your cell phone off
- Set a timer for the correct amount of time
- Use a pencil rather than a pen
- Try out all of the great tactics you've learned from this book!

You can find scantron-style answer sheets at the end of this book that you can tear out if you'd like to replicate the full test-taking experience.

For Practice Test 2, flip to the next page!

READING TEST

35 Minutes — 40 Questions

DIRECTIONS: There are four passages in this test. Each passage is followed by several questions. After reading a passage, choose the best answer to each question and fill in the corresponding oval on your answer document. You may refer to the passages as often as necessary.

Passage I

LITERARY NARRATIVE: This passage is adapted from the novel "Impressions Left" by Carol Filbin. (©2017 by Fox Literature).

Ben surveyed the spread of ingredients on the kitchen counter, grabbed the flour, and began to sift its tiny clumps into fine powder. His grandmother had already started heaving great slabs of butter into the bowl of the electric mixer for the buttercream frosting. Though her fingers, arthritic and knobbed, struggled to hold a pen or even press the numbers on her old phone, Grandma still handled her spatula like a pro. Patiently, making her way through the secret recipe she had used for all of Ben's birthdays, she prepared her frosting from scratch (only her own frosting, she said, could hold her intricate decorations). Here, at Hawthorn Meadows, she refused to give up any of her old traditions, and her recipes topped that list. She seemed content, Ben thought, or at least busy. But he also knew that Grandma missed her old sunny kitchen only a few miles away.

Ben thought fondly of that old place: not far in miles, unreachable in time. It had been a sanctuary, the warm neutrality of Grandma's kitchen inviolable no matter what childish fights roiled Forest Elementary. Even in the year Ben turned eight, when his birthday coincided with game 3 of the 4-game showdown between the White Sox and the Cubs, Grandma managed to unite everyone around the table. Ben's grandfather was a Cubs fan in White Sox country, and so, anxious though he was to admit it, Ben was too. All summer long, every kid wagered dollar bills, baseball cards, and even video games against his team. The other kids called Ben "the boy who was raised by Cubs." For Ben's birthday party, on the day the Cubs and White Sox met at Wrigley Field, Grandma made her famous cake trimmed in Cubs red and blue. It was a strawberry pound cake with buttercream icing, and it was such a revelation—"There's no way this is fruit!"—that no one even noticed they were dining with the enemy.

"Should we add some vanilla bean to the icing?" Grandma asked. Ben suddenly realized he was sifting an empty sieve.

"Of course," he said, brought back from his nostalgic reflections. "Aunt Rhonda loves your vanilla icing."

But his mind quickly wandered again. It was to be the first family celebration in the Hawthorn Meadows facility, and, despite her outward enthusiasm, Ben wasn't sure his Grandma was entirely excited about it. When all your children and grandchildren gather in this new place, this apartment that is supposedly now your home, does the change become irreversible? Ben wondered if, like him, Grandma was thinking back to those birthday parties on Walnut Avenue, back when she still baked to mark occasions in the middle, not the end, of a story.

One thing was for sure: her past year had been difficult. In the beginning, when her children came to her and asked her to move into the assisted living facility, she refused, agreeing only after the loss of her husband of 52 years, and following that, a bad fall that threatened her own independence. Ben suspected it was a concession, not a choice, to move—that Grandma had never truly felt ready to leave her home—and had only moved out of a growing fear of becoming a burden to her own children. In that moment, Ben was struck by the realization that his grandmother had lived her own, separate life, one full of her own thoughts and ideas, separate from the life she had lived as a mother, aunt, and grandmother. He tried to think of something to say, something to help encourage her to open up and tell her story.

"Grandma," he finally asked, searching for something simple to start with, "where did you learn all this? To bake, I mean?" He realized that, after a childhood spent sitting at her kitchen table, being peppered with questions about his friends and school, he knew much less about her than she knew about him.

"From my grandfather, Benjamin. You are named after him! When I was growing up, we couldn't afford the ingredients, so a cake was an extraordinary thing. We couldn't use eggs or milk, but we baked anyway, and I remember the first cake we made for your Great Uncle Bill's 3rd birthday had cornmeal mixed in with the flour and a little squiggle of an airplane I drew in chocolate syrup instead of frosting. Billy took one bite and threw it on the floor." Grandma laughed. "Love is an important ingredient, Ben, but it cannot replace eggs."

As Grandma now added one precise quarter cup of milk to the bowl, she sighed. These cakes, Ben saw, were for more than just the day's guests; they were for all those grandparents, and parents, and siblings Grandma carried around like so many secret recipes.

As Grandma put the finishing touches on the cake's icing, Ben answered a knock at the door.

"Georgia, come in!" Grandma shouted.

"Ben, this is Georgia from down the hall. Georgia, come take a look at my cake!"

Ben smiled. A friend to bake with. Maybe Grandma could do more here than just remember what had been.

1. The passage makes clear that for Ben's grandmother, baking is:

A. a beloved opportunity to bring together her family and friends.
B. a sought-after chance to show off her talents in search of praise and recognition.
C. a rare occasion, because she cannot afford the proper ingredients.
D. a once-loved activity that now makes her too nostalgic for happier times.

2. Which of the following events referred to in the passage occurred first chronologically?

F. Ben and his grandmother baked a cake together at Hawthorn Meadows.
G. Ben's grandmother baked a Cubs-themed birthday cake.
H. Ben's grandmother baked a cake for Great Uncle Bill.
J. Ben's grandmother baked a cake for Georgia.

3. The phrase "dining with the enemy" in line 34 most nearly refers to the fact that:

A. a family feud took place at Ben's birthday party.
B. Cubs baseball players were invited to Ben's birthday party, even though most of the guests were White Sox fans.
C. Ben and his grandmother got into a fight over the cake that she baked him for his birthday party.
D. the birthday cake Ben's grandmother baked was decorated in the colors of the baseball team that most guests at the party did not support.

4. The tone of the final sentence of the passage can best be described as:

F. hopeful and elated.
G. optimistic and reflective.
H. finite and pensive.
J. nostalgic and depressing.

5. According to the passage, Ben's grandmother has recently moved from:

A. The Cranberry Wing.
B. Walnut Avenue.
C. Hawthorn Meadows.
D. Wrigley Field.

6. It can most reasonably be inferred from the passage that Ben's grandmother moved from her house into the assisted living facility:

F. enthusiastically; she was excited to start the next chapter of her life.
G. readily; after a difficult year, she welcomed the support of a new living community.
H. reluctantly; she didn't want to, but she also didn't want to inconvenience her family.
J. unwillingly; she fought her family's decision but was ultimately forced to leave her home.

7. The word *inviolable* (line 19) most nearly means:

A. not breaking a law.
B. passive.
C. too sacred to be disrespected.
D. not dirty.

8. It can most reasonably be inferred from the passage that Ben is "sifting an empty sieve" (lines 36–37) because:

F. he is lost in his own thoughts and distracted by his memories.
G. he has never used a sieve before and doesn't know how to.
H. he has finished a step in the recipe and is waiting for further directions from Grandma.
J. he is bored while he waits to add vanilla bean to the cake's icing.

9. The passage indicates that Billy is:

A. Ben's three-year-old brother.
B. Grandma's cousin.
C. Grandma's grandfather.
D. Ben's great uncle.

10. The information in lines 72–80 serves primarily to:

F. provide an anecdote that is a treasured story from Ben's childhood.
G. give direct insight into Grandma's background through her own dialogue.
H. detail the occasion that solidified how Ben received his name.
J. explain why Grandma uses the ingredients that she does when she bakes.

Passage II

SOCIAL SCIENCE: Passage A is adapted from the article *Beringia* by Roberto Sacco. (©2018 by Scientific Notice). Passage B is adapted from the article *The Kelp Highway* by Florence Abbington. (©2017 by Scientific Notice).

Passage A by Roberto Sacco

About 20,000 years ago, at the height of the last Ice Age, any human journey from Asia to America would have been incredibly challenging, a harrowing trek across glaciers with nowhere to sleep except atop 5 the thick permafrost covering the continents. Nevertheless, foreboding as the trek might have been, human perseverance (and perhaps human desperation) might just have made it possible. At the glacial maximum, before the ice from that era began its slow retreat, low sea levels 10 exposed a visible land bridge linking Siberia and Alaska. The Bering Land Bridge, as it came to be known, could have enabled humans to walk the entire distance from Asia to North America.

The land on the Alaskan side of the bridge was 15 likely a more desirable place to live than icy Siberia, where humans had eked out an existence. The Alaskan climate was damper, and its land was covered in woody shrubs—vegetation that would have provided fuel for then-crucial fire. It's likely humans looked across the 20 bridge with some sense of possibility.

One common theory of human settlement of the Americas goes thus: from an icy Siberian home base, small groups of hunter-gatherers struck out into the new wilderness, following the migration of large grazing an-25 imals. These hunter-gatherers pressed forward, generation after generation, living in isolated groups that slowly progressed toward North America. Over thousands of years, they genetically diverged from the humans left behind, and by the time they arrived in the Americas, these 30 pioneers were a genetically distinct population. As the North American ice sheets began to melt, humans journeyed deeper into the vast American continent, establishing scattered civilizations, becoming who we now know as the Native Americans.

35 Their first known settlement, dating to 15,000 B.C.E., is today known as Clovis. Compellingly, a 2014 genetic study of a Clovis boy who died about 12,700 years ago seemed to confirm what scientists had hypothesized: the vast native populations of North and South 40 America all descended from a single, relatively small group of travelers who entered the North American continent by land. About 80% of Native Americans are direct descendants of the Clovis people.

However, recent studies have raised vexing ques-45 tions about the first migration. Some populations in South America's Amazon, for example, have been found to be genetically unrelated to the Clovis boy, suggesting that some people might have found their way to the Americas by a completely different path. In addition, 50 some Native Americans show more genetic similarities to people living on islands than to other native people of the Americas. These genetic mysteries have prompted scientists to continue research into the history and origin of the American peoples.

Passage B by Florence Abbington

55 For decades, history books have claimed that hunter-gatherers trekked across a vast icy wilderness, departing Siberia to become the first human inhabitants of the Americas. However, new research upends that simple narrative. While recent population studies confirm that 60 the Beringian Migration did, in fact, occur, they also suggest that long before any land bridge even started to appear, humans had already settled the North American continent.

Scientists now believe that the first humans to settle 65 the Americas arrived not by land, but by ocean, traveling via a coastal route that would have been navigable long before ice-age glaciers retreated sufficiently to allow for overland migration. On the edge of the north Pacific, from Asia to North America, a "kelp highway" 70 would have sustained abundant marine resources—kelp being an essential food source for marine life—and thus enabled the First Americans to arrive via boat.

Around 14,000 B.C.E., traveling eastward from Siberia along the northern Pacific Ocean coastline, 75 sailors would have had access to essential resources, including fish, shellfish, seabirds, and kelp, as well as the relative safety of protected natural harbors along the way. This Pacific Rim journey, as it came to be known, also explains how the first settlers arrived in Central Amer-80 ica, where people could have followed paths not of kelp, but of equally hospitable mangrove.

Archaeological evidence supports the theory of early maritime settlement of the Americas. The South American site of Monte Verde, for example, contains evi-85 dence of human settlement dating back 18,000 years. Researchers have also found evidence of humans in Florida dating back to 16,500 B.C.E. Both of these settlements predate the Bering Land Bridge by thousands of years.

Unfortunately, the coastal locations of early Ameri-90 can settlements would have left them vulnerable to natural erosion. In fact, over thousands of years, post-glacial sea rise has eroded American coastlines dramatically. Researchers are now investigating underwater locations, as well as select coastal areas where land has remained 95 relatively stable, hoping to unearth more support for the theory that the Americas were first widely settled not by hikers following a trail of game, but by seafarers following trails of kelp and mangrove.

Questions 11–13 ask about Passage A.

11. The author of Passage A most directly indicates that hunter-gatherers left Siberia because:

A. glaciers were taking over land where the hunter-gatherers hunted.
B. they wanted to become genetically distinct from their ancestors.
C. the Bering Land Bridge was a dangerous route.
D. they followed the migration of herds of animals.

12. In lines 44–52, the author of Passage A most likely discusses recent studies in order to:

F. provide examples to support conclusions about the Clovis people.
G. contrast the route taken by Native American ancestors to those in Asia.
H. transition from a popular theory to evidence that refutes the theory.
J. imply that all previous research on the Bering Land Bridge should be considered false.

13. In Passage A, the journey across the Bering Land Bridge can best be characterized as:

A. frightening; creatures hunted humans along the route.
B. practical; most humans in Siberia chose to make the journey to America.
C. impossible; no humans were likely able to complete the journey.
D. dangerous; frozen landscapes made travel difficult.

Questions 14–17 ask about Passage B.

14. Which of the following best describes the main idea of Passage B?

F. Migration to the Americas began when glaciers started to melt.
G. Research shows that early humans likely arrived in the Americas by sea.
H. Early humans arrived in the Americas by crossing a land bridge.
J. Kelp was an important food source for early humans traveling to the Americas.

15. According to Passage B, all of the following were essential to sailors traveling from Siberia EXCEPT:

A. fish.
B. protected harbors.
C. kelp.
D. mangrove.

16. The author of Passage B describes studies about the Beringian Migration in lines 58–63 primarily to:

F. contradict the theory that early Americans first arrived by a land route.
G. imply that all previous research into the early American population is false.
H. suggest that science is unable to prove how people traveled in 14,000 B.C.E.
J. provide evidence for the theory that early Americans arrived by sea.

17. It can reasonably be inferred from Passage B that present-day research to support the theory of sea travel to America is difficult to conduct because:

A. humans no longer inhabit the areas that were first settled.
B. researchers lack funding to study underwater locations.
C. the "kelp highway" is now used by modern boats rather than canoes.
D. erosion and sea rise changed the coastline over time.

Questions 18–20 ask about both passages.

18. Which of the following best captures a main difference between the two passages?

F. Passage A focuses on the impact of glaciers on early human civilization, while Passage B focuses on the geography of the continents 18,000 years ago.
G. Passage A focuses on the quality of life for settlers in the Americas, while Passage B focuses on the quality of life for humans who remained in Siberia.
H. Passage A focuses on the dates when humans first began to settle the Americas, while Passage B focuses on evidence from 16,500 B.C.E.
J. Passage A focuses on a common theory of human settlement of the Americas, while Passage B focuses on refuting that theory with new research.

19. The authors of both passages would most likely agree with which of the following statements?

A. Land bridges allowed humans to settle on islands.
B. Scientists have confirmed the method by which humans traveled to the Americas.
C. Kelp was an essential food source for early human settlers of the Americas.
D. Humans migrated across the Bering Land Bridge.

20. Compared to Passage B, Passage A provides more information regarding:

F. the years when humans likely settled in the Americas.
G. the resources available along the coastlines of the Americas.
H. reasons why human settlers left Siberia to travel to the Americas.
J. archeological evidence about human settlers of the Americas.

Passage III

HUMANITIES: This passage is adapted from the article "Jazz and Jon" by Pieter Crane. (©2017 by Music Music Music).

Dubbed the "James Joyce of jive" by Time Magazine, Jon Hendricks walked tall in the world of jazz for decades, rising from modest beginnings in his home state of Ohio to achieve an international fame rooted in his celebrated tours of America and Europe. Throughout his career, Hendricks maintained that his success was not a simple consequence of talent or even hard work, but rather an organic result of his deep love of music, instilled by his mother beginning the day he was born.

Though Jon was born in Newark, Ohio in 1921, the Hendricks family moved to Toledo in his early life. He was one of 14 siblings, the son of an African Methodist Episcopal pastor whose work would ultimately lay the foundation for his son's musical career. Hendricks' mother, Willie, sang in the choir; she brought home to Jon and his siblings the rhythmic elements and deep spiritual lyrics of traditional gospel. Hendricks was smitten. By the age of nine, he was singing regularly, and to local acclaim, at a roadhouse in his hometown. His charismatic voice was precise yet playfully improvisational, capable of gliding effortlessly between successive notes. Jon quickly became a local celebrity, and, by his teenage years, was singing on the radio with Art Tatum, a well-known jazz pianist and fellow Toledo native.

After serving in the Army during World War II, Hendricks entered college in hopes of becoming a lawyer. The pull of music, however, proved irresistible. After graduation, wary of his financial prospects yet trusting in his passion, Hendricks turned away from his original plan for law school in order to instead pursue his singing career in New York City.

Hendricks was known throughout his career for his work as a jazz lyricist, one who famed band leader Dizzy Gillespie called the "Poet Laureate of Jazz." Hendricks referenced a vast array of cultural and historical topics in his lyrics, from Shakespeare to the Spanish Civil War, but even more significant than their connection to history was their deep connection to the places and figures of the jazz world. In Hendricks' hit "Jumpin' at the Woodside" (the Woodside being a New York hotel popular among jazz musicians), the lyrics seem to leap from references to the city itself, through improvisational rhymes, and into abstractions of sound that suggest movement. The lyrics are simultaneously humorous and intelligent, drawing playful connections between images and ideas.

Hendricks was notable not only for the wording of his lyrics, but also for the way in which he paired lyrics with melodies. He was a pioneer of the "vocalese" form, which adds lyrics to already popular, often complex, instrumental jazz songs. The lyrics of vocalese work to enhance an instrumental solo and create a narrative, almost always in rhyme. Hendricks often wrote his lyrics to wild instrumental solos.

Hendricks' approach to creating vocalese lyrics was transformational in the world of jazz: he lent a new literary dimension to the music. Hendricks would take the time to discuss the meaning of a song with its composer and then would write lyrics that gave a narrative to each of the song's instruments: a plaintive saxophone or blaring trumpet, perhaps. The lyrics for each instrument would build on each other, fusing to create a single narrative that fit together like a puzzle.

In addition to his work as a lyricist, Hendricks was known for his scat singing, which derived from bebop, a style known for complicated musical compositions that became popular in the United States in the late 1940s. Scat singing allowed Hendricks to match the quick tempo and improvisations of bebop music note for note. Jazz journalist Leonard Feather compared Hendricks' voice to a "human horn."

Much of Hendricks' most famous work comes from his time as a member of the vocal jazz trio Lambert, Hendricks, and Ross. The group's first recording was multi-tracked, an innovative recording style that allowed each singer to record more than one track, a method that captured and amplified Hendricks' layered, maximalist approach to writing and singing. From 1957–1962, the trio was one of the most popular vocal groups in the world, touring the United States and Europe. In 1958, the group won a Grammy for Best Jazz Performance.

In his later years, Jon Hendricks worked in every corner of the music industry, demonstrating range that even his early musical promise may not have fully suggested. He sang with the group The Warlocks (later known as the Grateful Dead); worked as a music critic for the San Francisco Chronicle; taught jazz to students at the University of Toledo, California State University at Sonoma, and University of California at Berkeley; and wrote music for an off-Broadway musical.

Now a jazz legend, Jon Hendricks embodies the spirit of an era. His pioneering work in vocalese, poetic lyrics, and multi-tracked vocal album recording has earned him an honored, and rightful, place in music history.

21. The main purpose of the fifth paragraph (lines 47–54) is to:

A. contrast Hendricks' style with notable stylistic aspects of other famous jazz artists.
B. transition from a history of Hendricks' career to a discussion of specific details of his musical style.
C. introduce a musical technique for which Hendricks is known.
D. provide details about Hendricks' preferred musical instruments.

22. The passage most strongly suggests that Hendricks' most famous work comes from:

F. the music recorded as part of a vocal jazz trio.
G. collaborations with band leader Dizzy Gillespie.
H. spiritual lyrics he learned as part of a church choir.
J. his use of the vocalese technique.

23. One function of the author's list of Hendricks' work in his later years is to:

A. explain why Hendricks chose to eventually leave the world of jazz.
B. demonstrate the broad scope of Hendricks' musical influence.
C. prove that Hendricks was the best jazz musician of his era.
D. emphasize the importance of Hendricks' work in California.

24. The passage indicates that vocalese lyrics are used to:

F. create a new form of experimental jazz.
G. cross over from jazz into other music genres.
H. complement instrumental solos by adding rhyme and narrative.
J. give instrumentalists an alternate way to perform their work.

25. As it is used in line 77, the word *layered* most nearly means:

A. stratified.
B. enclosed.
C. multifaceted.
D. concealed.

26. Which of the following is NOT a characteristic of bebop?

F. Scat singing
G. Complicated musical composition
H. Improvisation
J. Quick tempo

27. In line 29, the word *passion* most nearly refers to:

A. advice from Hendricks' parents to get a steady job.
B. Hendricks' desire to become a musician.
C. Hendricks' willingness to become a lawyer.
D. Hendricks' long-term career in the Army.

28. The passage most clearly states that Hendricks' lyrics were inspired by:

F. culture and history.
G. his childhood in Ohio.
H. famous jazz musicians whom he admired.
J. different types of instruments popular in jazz music.

29. According to the passage, Hendricks' voice can best be described as:

A. contemporary.
B. peculiar.
C. serious.
D. precise.

30. The main idea of the first paragraph is that:

F. Hendricks' love of music inspired his long career.
G. Hendricks has many similarities to the famous novelist James Joyce.
H. Hendricks was a jazz musician who is forgotten in the modern era.
J. Hendricks believes musicians must work hard to achieve fame.

Passage IV

NATURAL SCIENCE: This passage is adapted from the article "Invasive Plants" by Victoria Schpiegl. (©2018 by *Scientific Journal of the Biodome*).

Stand at the edge of a Connecticut wetland or the banks of a Massachusetts river in July, and chances are you'll see a carpet of purple flowers tracing, sometimes in dense thickets, the meandering paths of water. It's a postcard-perfect image, one that appears in countless coffee table books and calendars—not to mention actual postcards—celebrating the natural splendor of old New England. But what the images invariably fail to capture is the danger hidden in the roots: all those brilliant highlights are the stalks of purple loosestrife, an invasive plant now threatening to strangle large swaths of the country's native wetlands. It is but one of thousands of similarly invasive species in the United States alone, many sharing parallel origin stories.

Like so much else in nature that is, at its core, deadly, many invasives possess a true surface-level beauty. In the case of loosestrife, it was intentionally imported to the United States as a striking ornamental accent for the gardens of European settlers. Its evolution from cultivated flower to renegade weed is typical of its invasive brethren: Settler imports plant to enjoy its beauty. Plant's seeds, unheeding of fences, spread by bird and wind beyond the garden. New plant colony spreads beyond settlers' control. And finally, dense wild thickets of now-entrenched weed render once-fertile ecosystems (many previously consisting of cattails) unsuitable as nesting or foraging habitats for waterfowl, fish, and other native wildlife.

Among other invasives, perhaps the most virulent is *Pueraria lobata*, more commonly known as kudzu, or colloquially as "the plant that ate the South." Its story serves as a cautionary tale of good intentions gone awry. The kudzu vine has the distinction of having been introduced not by European settlers, but by a foreign government: the nation of Japan, which made kudzu the centerpiece of its Japanese Pavilion at the Philadelphia Centennial Exposition in 1876. Visitors admired the vine's fragrant summer flowers, but also its remarkable ability to quickly establish a lush, cool canopy as a shield against the summer sun. They adopted kudzu as a climbing shade plant that must have seemed a marvelous international gift indeed, particularly in the sweltering American South.

But that was only the beginning of kudzu's American saga. Beginning in the early 1900s, the US government took advantage of another signature kudzu characteristic: its famously deep and intricate root systems, which can be used to counteract soil erosion. Faced with rapid loss of ground soil as farms expanded in size and scope, the government actually paid farmers to plant kudzu alongside their crops. By the 1930s, when the Dust Bowl threatened to decimate the nation's central farmlands, kudzu was being used extensively by the Civilian Conservation Corps as its primary weapon to reestablish some control over the landscape. Continuing into the 1940s, when the post-war expansion of cities, towns, and infrastructure resulted in intense deforestation along the coasts, the kudzu vine was again used by the US government to rapidly "re-green" the landscape. The Soil Conservation Service alone is estimated to have planted nearly one million acres of kudzu. At the time, kudzu must have seemed a true agricultural miracle: not only would the roots rapidly establish along the borders of farmland, but kudzu, a nitrogen-fixing plant, would also convert free nitrogen in the air into soil nitrates, a necessity for American crops.

The massively invasive, destructive qualities of the kudzu vine were, unfortunately, not discovered until the 1950s. What we now know is that the plant possesses a reproductive system almost perfectly evolved for alien invasion. The mature kudzu is capable of foot-a-day growth for up to 100 feet per year. The key to its success is its method of propagation: as the vine creeps horizontally along the forest floor, nodes anchor to exposed soil every few feet, planting massive tuberous roots called root crowns deep underground to effectively establish an entirely new plant. From each crown emerges a massive tangle of vine growing in every conceivable direction. The crowns, which can weigh hundreds of pounds each, store starches, water, and carbon reserves—vital resources that allow the kudzu to survive everything from drought years to fires to intensive human efforts at eradication. Even when the vine appears visually to be gone, it can re-emerge, sometimes years later.

Today, kudzu threatens native forests on the East Coast as far up as New York City, where the vine forms a particularly visible part of the landscape. As kudzu climbs native trees, it topples them by strangulation, or simply by the sheer power of its weight. And yet, to stand in the silent calm of a New York kudzu forest is to confront an inescapable irony. A short hike from any highway leads to the kudzu's alien preserve: a parallel metropolis of green monoliths spiralling upward, the expanse of tangled vines spreading ceaselessly in every direction. An invasive species intent on its own growth, propagation, domination: is the goal of the kudzu so distant from that of the city itself?

31. The main purpose of the passage is to use the example of kudzu to show:

A. the reasons that people choose to introduce new species to an area.
B. what steps scientists must take to eradicate purple loosestrife.
C. the qualities that allow kudzu to spread quickly and last for many years.
D. that the introduction of invasive plants has potentially harmful effects.

32. The passage indicates that the kudzu plant was initially introduced to the United States by:

F. the nation of Japan at the Philadelphia Centennial Exposition.
G. gardeners who wanted to bring a climbing plant to their gardens.
H. natural spreading methods, such as animals spreading seeds.
J. the Civilian Conservation Corps as a way to combat dusty soil.

33. The primary purpose of the second paragraph (lines 15–28) is to:

A. introduce the process through which an invasive species spreads in an ecosystem.
B. offer an overview of the types of plants and animals that are most harmed by invasive species.
C. present reasons why nonnative species should never be introduced in an ecosystem.
D. argue that birds should be used to control the spread of invasive species.

34. As it is used in line 92, the word *alien* most nearly means:

F. non-native.
G. extraneous.
H. universal.
J. unique.

35. Based on the passage, kudzu causes problems in New York because it:

A. establishes root systems deep underground.
B. climbs and strangles native trees.
C. has fragrant flowers that bloom in summer.
D. survives natural and human-caused fires.

36. The main idea of the fourth paragraph (lines 44–66) is that in the 1900s, kudzu was used:

F. as a shade plant in people's yards.
G. to counteract environmental issues with the landscape.
H. to support the reforestation of areas with trees that had been cut down.
J. to conserve rain in traditionally drought-laden areas.

37. The passage indicates that kudzu serves a necessary function for American crops by:

A. surviving drought years by storing water in its roots.
B. toppling native trees to clear space for farmland.
C. converting nitrogen in the air to nitrates in the soil.
D. establishing large tangles of vines to block sunlight from reaching the ground.

38. It can reasonably be inferred from the passage that the author describes purple loosestrife as "postcard-perfect" in line 5 in order to:

F. allow the reader to visualize a New England forest in the summer.
G. provide evidence to support the claim that the plant should be expunged from New England soil.
H. include a detail that contrasts the danger posed by the plant.
J. emphasize the vast area where the plant has spread.

39. Based on the passage, the initial decision to bring purple loosestrife and kudzu to the United States is best described as:

A. well-intentioned; people hoped to improve the soil by farming new plant species.
B. malicious; people disliked the native plants and wanted to replace them.
C. ignorant; people studied the potential impact of invasive species and ignored the results.
D. naive; people brought the plants for decoration but did not understand the potential consequences.

40. The passage indicates that one million acres of kudzu were planted by:

F. farmers in the Dust Bowl.
G. the Soil Conservation Service.
H. European settlers.
J. the Civilian Conservation Corps.

STOP: END OF TEST 2

6.1 Answer Key

<table>
<tr><th>Question Number</th><th>Correct Answer</th><th>Question Type</th><th>Question Tier</th></tr>
<tr><th colspan="4">LITERARY NARRATIVE</th></tr>
<tr><td>1</td><td>A</td><td>Main Idea</td><td>2</td></tr>
<tr><td colspan="4">A. Lines 82–85 reveal Ben's realization that Grandma makes cakes to connect with her own history, her family, and her friends.
B. The passage does not mention Grandma baking for praise or recognition.
C. Grandma's inability to afford ingredients is a detail that appears in an anecdote from her childhood, not the present tense.
D. Grandma may be nostalgic, but she still loves baking.</td></tr>
<tr><td>2</td><td>H</td><td>Specific Detail</td><td>3</td></tr>
<tr><td colspan="4">F. Events taking place at Hawthorn Meadows are the most recent events to take place chronologically.
G. The Cubs-themed birthday cake was an event from Ben's childhood, but not the earliest event among the answer choices.
H. Ben's grandmother baked a cake for Great Uncle Bill in her own childhood; it's how she first learned to bake, so it must be the earliest event in the story.
J. The passage does not mention Grandma baking a cake for her new friend Georgia, though it does mention Georgia seeing the cake Grandma has baked for her family.</td></tr>
<tr><td>3</td><td>D</td><td>Specific Detail</td><td>1</td></tr>
<tr><td colspan="4">Lines 30–31 state that "Grandma made her famous cake trimmed in Cubs red and blue." The cake was so delicious that the White Sox fans didn't notice that it was a Cubs cake.</td></tr>
<tr><td>4</td><td>G</td><td>Specific Detail</td><td>1</td></tr>
<tr><td colspan="4">"Optimistic" captures Ben's hope that Grandma will create new memories with new friends. "Reflective" accurately describes how Ben is asking thoughtful questions about how his Grandma will now live.</td></tr>
<tr><td>5</td><td>B</td><td>Specific Detail</td><td>2</td></tr>
<tr><td colspan="4">Walnut Avenue is mentioned at multiple points in the passage as the address of the house where Grandma lived before moving into the assisted living facility.</td></tr>
<tr><td>6</td><td>H</td><td>Specific Detail</td><td>2</td></tr>
<tr><td colspan="4">Lines 56–59 state that Grandma "never truly felt ready to leave her home," but that she had a "fear of becoming a burden to her own children."</td></tr>
<tr><td>7</td><td>C</td><td>Specific Detail</td><td>1</td></tr>
<tr><td colspan="4">Lines 18–20 state that "it had been a kind of sanctuary, the warm neutrality of Grandma's kitchen inviolable no matter what childish fights or petty grievances roiled Forest Elementary." In context, "inviolable" means that everyone deeply respects the neutrality of Grandma's home.</td></tr>
<tr><td>8</td><td>F</td><td>Specific Detail</td><td>1</td></tr>
<tr><td colspan="4">Lines 38–39 state that Ben was "brought back from his nostalgic reflections" when Grandma asked him a question.</td></tr>
<tr><td>9</td><td>D</td><td>Specific Detail</td><td>2</td></tr>
<tr><td colspan="4">In lines 74–76, Grandma says, "and I remember the first cake we made for your Great Uncle Bill's 3rd birthday. . . " indicating that Bill is Ben's great uncle.</td></tr>
</table>

<table>
<tr><th>Question Number</th><th>Correct Answer</th><th>Question Type</th><th>Question Tier</th></tr>
<tr><td>10</td><td>G</td><td>Purpose</td><td>1</td></tr>
<tr><td colspan="4">F. The anecdote is from Grandma's childhood, not Ben's.
G. The excerpt is a quotation—Grandma's own words—responding to Ben's question about how she learned so much about baking.
H. The quotation introduces a story about how Grandma learned to bake, not how Ben got his name.
J. Ingredients are a detail that appear but are not the main purpose of the anecdote.</td></tr>
<tr><td colspan="4">SOCIAL SCIENCE</td></tr>
<tr><td>11</td><td>D</td><td>Specific Detail</td><td>1</td></tr>
<tr><td colspan="4">Lines 22–25 state: "...from an icy Siberian home base, small groups of hunter-gatherers struck out into the new wilderness, following the migration of large grazing animals."</td></tr>
<tr><td>12</td><td>H</td><td>Purpose</td><td>2</td></tr>
<tr><td colspan="4">F. The examples do not support, but contradict, original conclusions about the Clovis people.
G. This is a detail mentioned in the paragraph but not the main purpose of discussing recent studies.
H. Lines 44–45 state that "However, recent studies have raised vexing questions about the first migration." By mentioning recent studies, the author transitions from a popular scientific theory, which is the essay's focus, to some new complicating evidence.
J. The new studies have only raised questions; "all previous research...should be considered false" is much too extreme.</td></tr>
<tr><td>13</td><td>D</td><td>Specific Detail</td><td>2</td></tr>
<tr><td colspan="4">Lines 2–5 state: "...any human journey from Asia to America would have been incredibly challenging, a harrowing trek across glaciers with nowhere to sleep except atop the thick permafrost...," indicating that the journey was dangerous because of frozen conditions.</td></tr>
<tr><td>14</td><td>G</td><td>Main Idea</td><td>2</td></tr>
<tr><td colspan="4">F. The passage, which argues for sea migration, only mentions melting glaciers in reference to the older theory of land migration.
G. Lines 96–98 state: "...the Americas were first widely settled not by hikers following a trail of game, but by seafarers following trails of kelp and mangrove." The passage argues that recent research indicates that the first Americans came by sea.
H. This answer summarizes the old theory, which the passage only mentions in order to argue against it.
J. Kelp as a food source is a detail, not the main idea of the passage.</td></tr>
<tr><td>15</td><td>D</td><td>Specific Detail</td><td>3</td></tr>
<tr><td colspan="4">A. Fish are on the list of "essential resources" in lines 75–77.
B. Protected harbors are on the list of "essential resources" in lines 75–77.
C. Kelp is on the list of "essential resources" in lines 75–77.
D. Mangrove is mentioned as a potential resource in the passage, but not as part of the list of "essential resources."</td></tr>
</table>

<table>
<tr><th>Question Number</th><th>Correct Answer</th><th>Question Type</th><th>Question Tier</th></tr>
<tr><td>16</td><td>F</td><td>Purpose</td><td>1</td></tr>
<tr><td colspan="4">F. Lines 55–59 state: “...history books have claimed that hunter-gatherers trekked across a vast icy wilderness...new research upends that simple narrative.” The author’s main purpose is to contradict the theory that early Americans first arrived by land.
G. The author acknowledges that new research agrees with previous research in some ways. All previous research is not false.
H. On the contrary, the passage suggests that science has made good progress in explaining how the earliest humans arrived in the Americas.
J. The particular studies mentioned do not provide any evidence that would point to the sea. They simply suggest earlier migrations somehow took place.</td></tr>
<tr><td>17</td><td>D</td><td>Specific Detail</td><td>2</td></tr>
<tr><td colspan="4">Lines 89–93 state: “Unfortunately, the coastal locations of early American settlements would have left them vulnerable to natural erosion...Researchers are thus now investigating underwater locations. . . ”</td></tr>
<tr><td>18</td><td>J</td><td>Main Idea</td><td>2</td></tr>
<tr><td colspan="4">F. Passage B does not focus on the geography of continents. Paragraph A mentions the impact of glaciers, but not as its primary focus, which is the theory of human migration.
G. The focus of passage A is not quality of life; it’s human migration. The focus of passage B is the settlement of the Americas, not Siberia.
H. These are accurate details from both passages but do not indicate the main focus of either passage.
J. Passage A focuses on the land-route migration theory, while Passage B focuses on new research indicating a sea-route.</td></tr>
<tr><td>19</td><td>D</td><td>Specific Detail</td><td>2</td></tr>
<tr><td colspan="4">Lines 59–60 in Passage B state: “While recent population studies confirm that the Beringian Migration did, in fact, occur. . . ” Both passages acknowledge that humans did migrate by land across the Bering Land Bridge. Passage B simply argues that other, earlier humans migrated by boat.</td></tr>
<tr><td>20</td><td>H</td><td>Main Idea</td><td>2</td></tr>
<tr><td colspan="4">F. Both passages discuss the years when humans likely settled in the Americas.
G. On the contrary, Passage B provides more information about coastal resources.
H. Passage B provides very little information regarding the reasons why human settlers travelled to the Americas in the first place.
J. Both passages provide archeological evidence about human settlers of the Americas.</td></tr>
<tr><td colspan="4">HUMANITIES</td></tr>
<tr><td>21</td><td>C</td><td>Purpose</td><td>1</td></tr>
<tr><td colspan="4">A. Hendricks is the only jazz artist named in the paragraph.
B. Hendricks’ career is not specifically mentioned in this paragraph.
C. The intro sentence describes a “notable” technique used by Hendricks.
D. The paragraph is about a style of singing and does not mention musical instruments.</td></tr>
<tr><td>22</td><td>F</td><td>Specific Detail</td><td>2</td></tr>
<tr><td colspan="4">Lines 72–74 state that “Much of Hendricks’ most famous work comes from his time as a member of the vocal jazz trio Lambert, Hendricks, and Ross.“</td></tr>
</table>

<table>
<tr><th>Question Number</th><th>Correct Answer</th><th>Question Type</th><th>Question Tier</th></tr>
<tr><td>23</td><td>B</td><td>Purpose</td><td>2</td></tr>
<tr><td colspan="4">A. Hendricks was still involved in jazz in his later years.
B. Paragraph 9 (lines 82–90) lists that Hendricks “sang,” “worked as a music critic,” “taught jazz,” and “wrote music,” showing a range of abilities.
C. “Prove” and “best” are extreme words that the passage cannot fully support.
D. Although some of the places mentioned in the list are in California, that is not the purpose of the list.</td></tr>
<tr><td>24</td><td>H</td><td>Specific Detail</td><td>2</td></tr>
<tr><td colspan="4">Lines 51–53 state that “The lyrics of vocalese work to enhance an instrumental solo and create a narrative, almost always in rhyme.”</td></tr>
<tr><td>25</td><td>C</td><td>Specific Detail</td><td>1</td></tr>
<tr><td colspan="4">The sentence indicates that the “multi-tracked” recording allowed for multiple singers on each track.</td></tr>
<tr><td>26</td><td>F</td><td>Specific Detail</td><td>3</td></tr>
<tr><td colspan="4">F. Lines 65–66 indicate that scat singing is derived from bebop but do not say that it is a characteristic.
G. Paragraph 7 mentions bebop, “known for complicated musical compositions.”
H. Paragraph 7 mentions the “improvisation of bebop music.”
J. Paragraph 7 mentions the “quick tempo” of bebop.</td></tr>
<tr><td>27</td><td>B</td><td>Specific Detail</td><td>1</td></tr>
<tr><td colspan="4">Lines 27–29 state that “The pull of music, however, proved irresistible” and that Hendricks went on to trust “in his passion...”</td></tr>
<tr><td>28</td><td>F</td><td>Specific Detail</td><td>2</td></tr>
<tr><td colspan="4">Lines 34–36 state that “Hendricks referenced a vast array of cultural and historical topics in his lyrics...”</td></tr>
<tr><td>29</td><td>D</td><td>Specific Detail</td><td>2</td></tr>
<tr><td colspan="4">Lines 19–21 state that “his charismatic voice was... precise yet playfully improvisational...”</td></tr>
<tr><td>30</td><td>F</td><td>Main Idea</td><td>1</td></tr>
<tr><td colspan="4">F. In the conclusion sentence, Hendricks explains that his success came from “his deep love of music.”
G. This is a detail rather than a main idea, and James Joyce is used as a metaphor rather than a comparison.
H. The paragraph indicates that Hendricks was popular for decades, so he is likely not forgotten today.
J. Hard work is a detail and not the main reason for Hendricks’ success.</td></tr>
<tr><td colspan="4">NATURAL SCIENCE</td></tr>
<tr><td>31</td><td>D</td><td>Purpose</td><td>2</td></tr>
<tr><td colspan="4">A. The introduction of kudzu is a detail in the passage, not the passage’s main purpose.
B. Purple loosestrife is an example in the passage, not the main purpose.
C. Although the qualities of kudzu are discussed, it is in the context of the dangers of invasive plants.
D. The intro paragraph discusses the “danger hidden in the roots” and mentions that there are “thousands of similarly invasive species in the United States alone.”</td></tr>
<tr><td>32</td><td>F</td><td>Specific Detail</td><td>2</td></tr>
<tr><td colspan="4">Lines 34–37 state that the kudzu vine was introduced “by a foreign government: the nation of Japan...at the Philadelphia Centennial Exposition...“</td></tr>
</table>

<table>
<tr><th>Question Number</th><th>Correct Answer</th><th>Question Type</th><th>Question Tier</th></tr>
<tr><td>33</td><td>A</td><td>Purpose</td><td>1</td></tr>
<tr><td colspan="4">A. The paragraph uses the example of purple loosestrife to illustrate how an invasive species spreads.
B. Although the paragraph lists “waterfowl, fish, and other native wildlife,” that is not the paragraph’s main purpose.
C. The paragraph uses examples of invasive species but does not prove that nonnative species should never be introduced.
D. Birds are mentioned as a vehicle to spread invasive species, not control them.</td></tr>
<tr><td>34</td><td>F</td><td>Specific Detail</td><td>1</td></tr>
<tr><td colspan="4">Kudzu, introduced in lines 33–35, is described as being “introduced” by a “foreign government.”</td></tr>
<tr><td>35</td><td>B</td><td>Specific Detail</td><td>2</td></tr>
<tr><td colspan="4">Lines 87–88 state that “As kudzu climbs native trees, it topples them by strangulation...”</td></tr>
<tr><td>36</td><td>G</td><td>Main Idea</td><td>1</td></tr>
<tr><td colspan="4">F. This is not a detail from Paragraph 4.
G. Line 48 states that kudzu was used “to counteract soil erosion.” Line 59 states that kudzu was used to “‘re-green’ the landscape.”
H. The mention of kudzu helping deforested areas is a detail, not the main idea of the paragraph.
J. The paragraph does not mention rain.</td></tr>
<tr><td>37</td><td>C</td><td>Specific Detail</td><td>2</td></tr>
<tr><td colspan="4">Lines 64–66 state that kudzu, “a nitrogen-fixing plant, would also convert free nitrogen in the air into soil nitrates, a necessity for American crops.”</td></tr>
<tr><td>38</td><td>H</td><td>Purpose</td><td>1</td></tr>
<tr><td colspan="4">F. While the detailed description does allow the reader to visualize, the purpose is to contrast with the plant’s dangerous nature.
G. The description does not provide evidence about eliminating the plant.
H. In lines 8–9, the author contrasts the beauty of the purple loosestrife by stating, “But what the images invariably fail to capture is the danger hidden in the roots...”
J. The purpose of the description is not to emphasize the area where the plant has spread.</td></tr>
<tr><td>39</td><td>D</td><td>Specific Detail</td><td>2</td></tr>
<tr><td colspan="4">Lines 17–19 state that loosestrife “was intentionally imported to the United States as a striking ornamental accent for the gardens of European settlers.” Lines 40–41 indicate that people adopted kudzu “as a climbing shade plant...” These indicate that the plants were decorative, but that those who planted them did not understand the consequences of invasive species.</td></tr>
<tr><td>40</td><td>G</td><td>Specific Detail</td><td>2</td></tr>
<tr><td colspan="4">Lines 60–61 state that “The Soil Conservation Service alone is estimated to have planted nearly one million acres of kudzu.”</td></tr>
</table>

Raw Score: ___ / 40

Converted Score: ___ / 36

6.2 Scoring Rubric

Score Conversion[1]

Scaled Score	Raw Score	Raw Score	Scaled Score
1	0	19	**19**
2	–	20–21	**20**
3	1	22	**21**
4	2	23–24	**22**
5	–	25	**23**
6	3	26	**24**
7	–	27	**25**
8	4	28	**26**
9	5	29	**27**
10	6	30	**28**
11	7	31	**29**
12	8–9	32	**30**
13	10–11	33	**31**
14	12	34–35	**32**
15	13–14	36	**33**
16	15	37	**34**
17	16	38	**35**
18	17–18	39–40	**36**

[1]Score Conversions are general estimates based on the average correlations between raw scores and scaled scores as seen on recent ACT exams. They are meant to be used as such: general estimates.

Chapter 7

Practice Test 3

Remember to...

- Find a quiet space to work with limited distractions
- Turn your cell phone off
- Set a timer for the correct amount of time
- Use a pencil rather than a pen
- Try out all of the great tactics you've learned from this book!

You can find scantron-style answer sheets at the end of this book that you can tear out if you'd like to replicate the full test-taking experience.

For Practice Test 3, flip to the next page!

READING TEST

35 Minutes — 40 Questions

DIRECTIONS: There are four passages in this test. Each passage is followed by several questions. After reading a passage, choose the best answer to each question and fill in the corresponding oval on your answer document. You may refer to the passages as often as necessary.

Passage I

LITERARY NARRATIVE: This passage is adapted from the short story "Jane" by Franklin Dodger. (©2017 by Banks Literature).

Jane was nervous. That jittery sort of nervous, where you jump too high at the clatter of the cat knocking your chapstick off of the nightstand, where your stomach flutters at every errant thought. She hated this feeling, this uneasiness she couldn't shake, no matter how hard she tried, year after year. The cycle was as predictable as it was endless. About the only thing she could think to do to calm herself was to indulge in yet another step in the old routine: she could arrange and sharpen her new box of pencils, their slim golden lines fitting neatly into her slim golden hands as she pushed them into the mechanical sharpener. Its whirring, unfortunately, was not loud enough to drown out her rattling nerves.

Yes, it was another end, another beginning: the true, organic year, somehow unmarked on the calendars that made such an ado about January 1. It had been another wonderful summer. But weren't all summers wonderful? Weeks and weeks of open schedules, with no greater worry than to remember the sunscreen if the light of some lazy afternoon felt just bright enough to burn. She had spent so many of those lazy afternoons in the backyard, doing nothing but soaking in the warmth of the sun. Stretched motionless by the pool until she couldn't bear the heat any longer, she replaced drops of sweat with drops of icy water, a few swift laps, horizontal strokes running the length of the lane, enough to cool her down.

But this summer had been particularly lovely. Hadn't it? She had taken that fabulous trip to Barcelona with Sarah and Nguyen. Days spent by the seaside, nights spent on rooftops, their laughter echoing off the cobblestones of which the entire city seemed to be constructed. Jane's mother had been so worried the trip was "reckless" (Mom's favorite word of disapproval, as though you were wrecking the very idea of the person you were supposed to be). "How reckless! None of you speak Spanish! How reckless! Where on earth will you stay? How reckless..." But, as was always the case, the first "reckless" was enough for Jane to know she would be getting on that plane. She may have inherited her mother's nerves, but at least she tried to fight them. Her stubbornness rivaled that of even her brother Jack, whose "iron will" (her mother's description) always made Jane think of an armored knight.

Now everything was arranged precisely in her backpack. The fresh spirals of her notebooks were not yet entangled in errant paperclips and debris. Each pen was still a carefully-capped precision instrument, not yet the open-topped barb it would become, leaving polka dots on every book and paper inside.

So why was the first day of school always so tough?

Jane had tried to answer this question year after year. It was inexplicable: you knew what your schedule was and you knew who was in your classes. You knew what supplies you needed and you knew what you'd be eating for lunch on the first day, because you'd packed it yourself. You knew what time you'd wake up (but what if you missed the alarm?!). And you knew how you were getting there (but what if the bus was late?!). And yet routine offered no reassurance.

Maybe, Jane thought, part of the struggle came from mourning the loss of summer. Already, her tan was beginning to fade. Over the last few weeks, she'd sacrificed her mornings to long trips to Staples and Target, trading laps in the pool for laps through aisles of stationery.

Jane knew that her nerves were silly, but that made her feel even worse. The more she thought about how irrational they were, the more frustrated she felt that she couldn't control them. An awful cycle. It was the same as when you had a major paper that you hadn't even started. You would be so stressed about the amount of work that needed to be done, you just couldn't even start to do it—the thought of that blank white sheet was so terrifying that it was easier in the moment to push it away.

As she lay in bed, willing herself to crawl out from underneath the covers, to start yet another year, her phone began to vibrate from her bedside table. She reached out, the glow of the screen like a halo around the familiar name waiting for her to answer.

She set the phone on speaker beside her.

"Morning, Jane!" it said.

"Hey, Sarah. Still trying to get out of bed here."

"I wouldn't have expected anything less. You are the queen of the sleep-in. Anyway, I already did the Starbucks run, so don't stop on the way in. Your coffee will be waiting for you."

The voice, more than the promise of any caffeine, awoke in Jane some kernel of inspiration.

"I'll see you in homeroom," she said. "Home, room," she thought, turning in her mind the funny contours of that hopeful phrase.

1. The structure of the passage can best be described as a story in which the narrator:
   - **A.** uses first-person point of view to explain her feelings about going back to school.
   - **B.** describes the feelings of multiple characters about returning to school.
   - **C.** provides details about the family dynamics of a main character.
   - **D.** reflects on a main character's previous few months through flashbacks.

2. The example of pushing away a blank white sheet of paper most strongly supports which of the following statements about Jane?
   - **F.** "But this summer had been particularly lovely" (line 27)
   - **G.** "She'd sacrificed her mornings to long trips to Staples and Target" (lines 62–63)
   - **H.** "Jane knew that her nerves were silly, but that made her feel even worse" (lines 65–66).
   - **J.** "The voice, more than the promise of any caffeine, awoke in Jane some lost kernel of inspiration" (lines 86–87)

3. The passage indicates that a step in Jane's pre-school year routine is to:
   - **A.** float in her backyard pool.
   - **B.** purchase new packages of chapstick.
   - **C.** take a summer trip with friends.
   - **D.** sharpen pencils with a mechanical sharpener.

4. Based on the passage, Jane's feelings about returning to school at the end of the summer can best be described as:
   - **F.** unhappy and frantic.
   - **G.** anxious and tense.
   - **H.** thrilled and prepared.
   - **J.** reckless and disapproving.

5. The main purpose of the description of Jane's pens in lines 46–49 is to:
   - **A.** imply that Jane is incapable of keeping her school supplies neat.
   - **B.** provide an example of why Jane is dreading going back to school.
   - **C.** emphasize the meticulous arrangement of her backpack.
   - **D.** illustrate the polka dots that would be on each book.

6. The dialogue from Jane's mother in the passage most strongly suggests that she thought the trip to Barcelona was:
   - **F.** careless; she thought Jane should be preparing to go to school instead.
   - **G.** irresponsible; however, Jane decided to go anyway.
   - **H.** exciting; she was jealous that she did not get to go with Jane.
   - **J.** frustrating; this caused Jane to realize how poorly planned the trip was.

7. The primary purpose of the second paragraph (lines 14–26 is to:
   - **A.** describe Jane's typical weekly schedule.
   - **B.** provide details about Jane's summer job working at a pool.
   - **C.** challenge the reasoning for starting yearly calendars in January.
   - **D.** convey the relaxing nature of summer.

8. The passage makes clear that the first day of school is difficult for Jane in part because:
   - **F.** she is mourning the end of summer.
   - **G.** the school year starts in January rather than the fall.
   - **H.** she would rather spend her mornings shopping at Staples and Target.
   - **J.** she does not have the school supplies she needs to bring.

9. The main idea of the sixth paragraph (lines 51–59) is that:
   - **A.** Jane needs to wake up at a certain time to make it to school.
   - **B.** Jane wonders who her classmates will be in the fall.
   - **C.** Jane needs to find out which bus to take to get to school.
   - **D.** Jane is still nervous despite being prepared.

10. In the passage, Jane's brother Jack is described as:
    - **F.** her older sibling.
    - **G.** wearing armor.
    - **H.** having an iron will.
    - **J.** working as a knight.

Passage II

SOCIAL SCIENCE: This passage is adapted from the article "Peaceful Inklings " by David Valentino. (©2017 by Policy Matters Today).

Human civilization's capacity for good is extraordinary, matched only by its tendency toward evil. Given the history of the species, rife with both social and cultural achievement and political violence, will it ever be possible to maximize our positive and minimize our negative capacities? The question has long perplexed both social and political scientists, many of whom have chased an elusive ideal: to formulate a robust, universal theory of human political organization that can not only describe, but also shape the political organization of people. Perhaps, these scientists hope, the right theory will allow us to bend the arc of history toward a better future for all.

Democratic Peace Theory is a contender for one such universalizing theory, perhaps the most widely studied (and debated) in contemporary political science. Its basic premise is deceptively simple: democracies, as a direct effect of their democratic institutions and ideals (think parliaments, courts, congresses), are unlikely to go to war with other democracies. Consequently, the goal of existing democracies should be to devote power and resources to the creation and growth of other democracies globally, a strategy that will lead to greater interconnectedness and peace over time. The theory has gained a strong foothold in universities, as well as amongst diplomats, though it is not without its detractors. For while most political scientists agree that evidence supports a correlation between peace and democracy, it is unclear whether peace is caused by, or merely correlated with, democratic political organization.

If peace is, indeed, an inherent consequence of democracy, then the rules of international relations could be summarized fairly succinctly: spread democracy, and consequently, reduce warfare globally. A world of democracies might even do away with warfare altogether. This general premise is not a bad summary of the ideals, if not always the actions, that have governed Western international relations since World War II.

Can the relationship between democracy and peace really be so straightforward? The theory's central conceit may at first seem to suggest that democracies are inherently more peaceful than other nations. But Democratic Peace Theory makes no such claim, and rightly so. A cursory examination of history reveals numerous examples of violent upheavals both within and between democracies. The 20th century is replete with conflict, even violence, resulting from disputes between democratic nations. The claim, however, is not that democracies are generally peaceful, but rather that conflicts between democracies rarely escalate into true warfare.

But some political scientists and historians disagree even with the fundamental premise of Democratic Peace Theory. Examining the relations between nations over time, they do not see a history of peace between democracies, but rather a history of peace between wealthy, powerful nations that just so happen to be democratic. Seeing wealth, not political institutions, as the decisive factor in international relations, these critics remain skeptical that spreading democracy into non-democratic, often poorer parts of the world, would suffice to reduce world conflict.

Most criticism of Democratic Peace Theory falls under the category of political realism, the assumption that nations are driven by considerations of security and survival above all else. Political realism, as applied to international relations, argues that the power of democracies to influence conflict is in fact extremely limited. Democracies may be capable of influencing economic priorities and social ideals domestically, but not, in the end, the essential calculus that has for centuries either averted or necessitated war: maximizing access to limited resources. The idea that a democracy, regardless of who is in power, would not first and foremost seek survival and security is naïve.

The utility of Democratic Peace Theory can withstand at least some of the criticism. Even if the link between democracy and peace proves to be merely correlative, not causative, studying international relations between democracies could still help to identify some of the critical factors that lead to peaceful relations. Perhaps peace depends more on economics: maybe market economies are unlikely to go to war with other market economies to whom they are interconnected. Or perhaps peace depends more on culture: maybe countries that share and exchange popular cultures and ideas are unlikely to allow conflict to progress into warfare.

The answer as to why democracies do not go to war with other democracies remains elusive at best. Further research into the topic may prove that democracy and peace are intrinsically bound together, or that peace is a mere byproduct of some democratic ideal, or, alternatively, that any link between the two is mere coincidence. Perhaps continued study of Democratic Peace Theory will someday reveal the causes of an unfortunate, ironic truth: democracies, while maintaining peace with one another, have become notoriously skilled at fighting and winning wars with the non-democratic nations of the world.

11. Which of the following statements best captures the main idea of the passage?

A. Peace is only attainable for economically advantaged countries.
B. Despite concerted efforts, Democratic Peace Theory has failed to explain the history of the 20th century.
C. Democratic Peace Theory is a hypothesis that merits further study.
D. Societies must find the optimal balance between war and peace.

12. In the passage, the primary purpose of the question in lines 39–40 is to:

F. summarize the positive and negative events that make up human history.
G. offer an overview of the best ways for democracies to promote peace in the world.
H. introduce a question that Democratic Peace Theory seeks to address.
J. argue against the violence that is prevalent in interactions between governments.

13. As it is used in line 70, the word *averted* most nearly means:

A. avoided.
B. required.
C. predicted.
D. hid.

14. The passage strongly implies that international relations since World War II have been influenced by which of the following assumptions?

F. Democratic Peace Theory should guide governments' choices.
G. Peace is only possible among countries that support each other economically.
H. Governments will always be capable of taking advantage of one another.
J. Encouraging the development of democratic governments could reduce warfare globally.

15. According to the passage, Democratic Peace Theory makes the claim that:

A. market economies are less likely to go to war with each other.
B. democratic nations maintain peace with each other while fighting with non-democratic nations.
C. conflicts between democracies rarely escalate to war.
D. democracies tend to be more wealthy and powerful than non-democracies.

16. According to the passage, critics of Democratic Peace Theory characterize those who ignore the primacy of survival and security as:

F. realistic.
G. unethical.
H. unrealistic.
J. intelligent.

17. The passage indicates that Democratic Peace Theory has the strongest support among:

A. heads of state of major world powers.
B. political scientists and economists.
C. professors and diplomats.
D. politicians at the state and national level.

18. The passage mentions all of the following as potential contributing factors to peace between nations EXCEPT:

F. economics.
G. scholarship.
H. culture.
J. democracy.

19. The main purpose of the fifth paragraph (lines 51–61) is to:

A. transition to a discussion of the faults of Democratic Peace Theory.
B. provide counterexamples of countries that are not democracies.
C. contrast Democratic Peace Theory with other popular ideas in the field of international relations.
D. prove that democracies cannot survive in economically disadvantaged areas.

20. According to the passage, the 20th century provides examples of:

F. conflict based on class differences.
G. democratic nations protecting their non-democratic neighbors.
H. conflict and violence between democratic nations.
J. warfare taking place between non-democratic countries.

Passage III

HUMANITIES: Passage A is adapted from the article *Creation* by Francis Braun. (©2018 by Composer Biweekly). Passage B is adapted from the article *Musical Boundaries or Global Sound* by Terrance Reppert. (©2017 by Composition and Notes).

Passage A by Francis Braun

I usually begin my process in what may outwardly appear to be peaceful stasis. Sitting somewhere quiet, like a damp bench in Central Park, I close my eyes, slow my breathing, and wait. I listen for the muses to answer my silent request. Beneath a calm exterior, my mind is racing. My thoughts wander aimlessly across the landscape, across time. In this meditative space, after minutes that feel like hours, the city begins to speak to me: the laughter and chatter of passersby, the cacophony of traffic, the bird calls all intertwine, and noise becomes melody.

It is perhaps unsurprising that the muses of Central Park reveal music that so deeply evokes my home city: geography and musical composition have always been intrinsically linked for both creator and listener. In every composition—whether a classical cantata by the German Bach or a jazz arrangement by the American Duke Ellington—I hear in the structure, melody, and instrumentation some hint of the composer's nation, his travels, even the streets where he has lived. A symphony lays bare the history of its composer, every history but an amalgam of experience, each experience a product of environment.

Consciously or not, music is deeply rooted not only in landscape, but also in culture. A modern Czech symphony might unknowingly draw on the structure of a polka, while a composer from the Dominican Republic may incorporate the warmth of a bachata. The origin of a piece captures a part of that composer's identity at that moment in time. This observation that origins matter is intended not to impose restrictions, but rather to reveal possibility: travel and experience broaden the scope of musicians' imaginations, leading their work beyond the borders of their homes. Still, that original culture does establish deep and enduring roots that course through every composer's work.

In my own compositions, the translations from location and culture to composition are more literal than for most: a clanging trash can or a New York taxi horn might find its way, without filter, to the symphony hall. But it is important to emphasize that in creating such direct connections between place and music, I aim not to delineate, but rather to transcend, geographic borders. Sounds that are specific become universal. My compositions, I'm told, are distinctly of New York. And yet, because of their intimate link to the city, I hope my sounds can travel the world.

Passage B by Terrance Reppert

To transcend borders, a novel must be translated, and thus, transformed. The author's original creation is unlikely to survive intact. Visual art fares little better against the barriers of time and space: images stripped of context or explanation are stripped also of original meaning. Then there is music, especially wordless melody. A composition performed in any nation at any time seems to pull at the same heartstrings, instill the same fear, inspire the same euphoria as the day it was first performed. Might music be the world's one truly universal art?

Many critics point to melody's ability to move effortlessly across the globe as evidence of its universality. Even when composers align their work intimately with national identity, their music seems defiantly unbound by its original borders. Take the Russian symphonies of Rachmaninov or the Norwegian dances by Grieg as telling examples. Works composed for St. Petersburg and Oslo play to equal acclaim in London and New York.

The phenomenon of universality seems to hold equally for those contemporary compositions aligned intimately with geographic and national place. The composer Monica Sayles, for example, cites her home in Northern California as both the direct inspiration for and silent partner in her compositions. Her music belongs to the locations from which it was borne, the silences of the redwoods surrounding her home becoming the spaces between the notes in her compositions. Yet even these peculiar works achieve, without conscious intent, a universal appeal. Sayles has watched symphony orchestras from Asia to America perform her work, and her California compositions have achieved worldwide critical acclaim.

How, then, can a symphony written to reflect the soundscape of a western redwood forest connect deeply with listeners who have never been to the United States, let alone the remote northern coast of California? The answer relies heavily on the malleability of feeling. Compositions need not survive their travel through time and place entirely intact in order to be deeply felt.

The truth is, music may not be any more "universal" than the other arts. The feelings it evokes are indeed profoundly universal—the joy, the disquiet, the tranquility—not so the specificity of meaning, of musical reference, of musical narrative, or even the ideas that are the foundation of many compositions. For these layers, as with other forms of art, only scholarship, research, and explanation can illuminate the full intent and content of a composition. From this perspective, music is not so different from a work of visual art, or, acknowledging the necessary assistance of a translator, a book.

To be sure, some crucial element of music crosses boundaries. Melody's ability to circumvent literal thought and tap directly into emotion lends music its seeming universality. But in the absence of any explanation or context from the composer, music is just like the written and visual arts: art opens the door to experience, but it cannot control its message.

Questions 21–23 ask about Passage A.

21. The author of Passage A includes all of the following as examples of sounds in New York City EXCEPT:

A. taxi horns.
B. people talking.
C. polka instruments.
D. bird songs.

22. As it is used in line 21, the phrase "lays bare" most nearly means:

F. dissects.
G. reveals.
H. provides.
J. encounters.

23. In Passage A, the author most likely references Czech and Dominican music as examples of:

A. musicians broadening their horizons by traveling.
B. music composed in New York City having a more unique sound than music composed any other place.
C. musicians' cultures influencing the music they compose.
D. popular composers coming from all over the world.

Questions 23–26 ask about Passage B.

24. As she is presented in Passage B, Monica Sayles most clearly indicates that she believes her music to be:

F. best performed by orchestras in California.
G. dominated by the silences between notes.
H. less universal than older styles of music.
J. directly influenced by where she lives.

25. The author of Passage B most likely includes the references to the cities in lines 64–65 primarily to:

A. imply that the critical response to music depends on where it was composed.
B. give examples of famous compositions by artists around the world.
C. provide examples of music's ability to find appeal outside its place of origin.
D. emphasize the differences between music composed in different locations.

26. According to Passage B, novels tend to be viewed as less universal than musical compositions because:

F. people must understand their context.
G. they cause readers to feel fear and euphoria.
H. novelists lack the life experience to create books that transcend borders.
J. they must be translated for other audiences.

27. It can reasonably be inferred that the author of Passage B believes that the main reason music is considered to be more universal than other art forms is that music:

A. depends more on the context in which it was written.
B. allows listeners to feel emotion directly.
C. has a single correct interpretation.
D. is the only art form that can cause people to feel joy.

Questions 28–30 ask about both passages.

28. Which of the following statements best captures a primary difference in the focus of the two passages?

F. Passage A focuses on the experiences of a particular composer, while Passage B focuses on music in relation to other art forms.
G. Passage A focuses on the universality of music, while Passage B focuses on how music exists in a particular context.
H. Passage A focuses on music composed in New York, while Passage B focuses on music composed in California.
J. Passage A focuses on the audiences who enjoy symphonies, while Passage B focuses on critics of symphonies.

29. Compared to Passage B, Passage A provides more information regarding how music:

A. incites the same emotions across disparate audiences.
B. is more universal than other types of art.
C. is innately connected to nature.
D. can include sounds that aren't traditionally associated with symphonies.

30. Both passages support the idea that music linked closely to a particular location can result in:

F. a musical narrative limited by its composer's place of origin.
G. a universal sound that can have an impact outside its place of origin.
H. the use of sounds reminiscent of a particular city.
J. cultural differences between types of music.

Passage IV

NATURAL SCIENCE: This passage is adapted from the article "Bird Migration" by Edward Varmington. (©2018 by Scientific Journal of the Biodome).

For hundreds of thousands of years, the Earth's greatest navigators have kept their methods secret. Even today, we don't quite understand how they have managed their feats of endurance and mapping. Their names are peculiar, sometimes eccentric: the Sooty Shearwater (travels 40,000 miles a year from the Falkland Islands to the Arctic), the Bar-tailed Godwit (flies over 7,000 miles non-stop from Alaska to New Zealand), the Arctic Tern (travels an astonishing 44,000 miles annually on its migration from Arctic Greenland to the Antarctic Weddell Sea). Forget Columbus: when it comes to navigation, the true experts are our neighbors in the sky.

So how do birds do what they do? After centuries of study, most theories of avian navigation adhere to some version of what is known as the "map and compass" model, where a "compass" allows birds to orient themselves relative to the Earth's North-South axis and a "map" allows them to locate their bodily position relative to a home loft. Researchers broadly agree on the basic mechanism behind the "compass." In the daytime, birds can navigate by the position of the sun and at night by the rotation of the stars around some fixed point (usually the North Star.) In the absence of any reference light at all, such as occurs most dramatically during overcast nights, the compass still works: migratory birds can follow the North-South axis of the Earth by sensing the magnetism of its poles. But how does the "map" work? How do birds recognize their longitudinal and latitudinal positions relative to home? While the mechanisms behind the compass feature, which allow birds to travel in a fixed direction, are well-explained, the underlying mechanisms of the map feature remain widely debated.

In studies of bird geolocation, scientists have focused on the behavior of the homing pigeon, a species whose navigational abilities have earned it an outsized role in human history. Equipped with an uncanny instinct and ability to return to its home nest, the carrier pigeon, a tiny note often affixed to its leg, has served through centuries as the winged Mercury of human affairs, carrying secrets ranging from the invasions of Genghis Khan to news of the early Greek Olympic games to codes from Allied forces invading Normandy during World War I.

To study how the pigeons are able to reliably return home across great distances from unfamiliar drop-points, scientists look not to their navigational success, but rather to controlled studies of their navigational failures. By manipulating the ambient sensory information available to pigeons, and subsequently probing the resulting directional errors in flight, ornithologists attempt to pinpoint the sensory data birds must utilize in navigation. Navigational errors known as release-site bias are thus key to understanding how homing pigeons—and, by extension, all migratory birds—map their world.

One recent theory suggests that the key piece of sensory data for bird navigation is low-frequency sound waves. Called infrasound, these waves may allow pigeons to construct "audio maps" of their surroundings. Whereas humans are limited to sound ranges from about 20–20,000 hertz, pigeons are able to hear sounds as low as 0.05 Hz, well below the 0.1 to 0.2 Hz range in which infrasounds occur. When infrasound is disrupted through either natural or artificial means, the homing pigeons' ability to navigate home through the resulting "sound shadow" is significantly diminished. This could explain why pigeons often lose their way during periods of high wind or in the vicinity of supersonic jets.

Many ornithologists caution, however, that infrasound may be only one input in a vast array of sensory information utilized by birds. Other research suggests that birds utilize their sense of the Earth's magnetic field, which increases systematically from the equator toward the poles, as both compass and map. Birds may be able to determine not only the North-South axis, but also latitudinal position. Combined with an ability to sense regional variations in magnetization, migratory birds could theoretically map the world position of their home nests. But magnetic field detection is also not the whole picture. When a recent study pitted a loss of magnetic sense against a loss of smell in homing pigeons, those birds deprived of smell lost their navigational ability, but the birds deprived of magnetic sense successfully returned home. This information suggests that homing pigeons may, it seems, be capable of orienting themselves according to the position and density of odors, a skill known as olfactory navigation.

These seemingly competing theories may, in fact, all be true: different birds may use different senses to navigate in different circumstances. Sound, landmarks, smell, and magnetism can best be thought of as the raw sensory input birds can perceive. The senses they use depend on circumstance. Like a human feeling their way through a dark room or searching for the location of a bad odor or reading a map in an unfamiliar city, it is likely that a bird can utilize a wealth of sensory input to chart and navigate its world.

31. One of the main purposes of the passage is to show:

A. how infrasound allows birds to map their surroundings.
B. the different types of sensory input birds use to navigate.
C. the importance of birds in carrying messages.
D. which birds are able to navigate the longest distances.

32. The passage indicates that scientists studied pigeons' ability to return to their homes by:

F. looking at cases when the birds failed to navigate successfully.
G. measuring how the birds mapped a particular region.
H. researching stories of pigeons in history.
J. placing obstacles on the birds' routes back to their nests.

33. In the passage, the primary purpose of the second paragraph (lines 13–32) is to:

A. prove that birds use a compass to navigate.
B. introduce a basic theory that is expanded upon later in the passage.
C. summarize a study of how birds are able to locate their home nests.
D. present a theory that is later refuted and replaced with a new theory.

34. In the passage, all of the following are mentioned as messages that have been carried by pigeons EXCEPT:

F. news of Olympic games.
G. invasions of Genghis Khan.
H. maps of geographical features.
J. codes during World War I.

35. It can reasonably be inferred from the passage that birds' abilities to navigate directionally (as though with a compass) are:

A. what allow them to travel along lines of latitude and longitude.
B. difficult for scientists to reliably and accurately study.
C. related to use of low-frequency sound waves.
D. better understood than their ability to recognize their location.

36. As it is used in line 57, the word *construct* most nearly means:

F. create.
G. constrain.
H. eradicate.
J. write.

37. Based on the passage, a disruption to infrasound most nearly causes:

A. high winds and supersonic noises.
B. a weakening of pigeons' navigational abilities.
C. changes in Earth's magnetic fields.
D. birds to create audio maps of their surroundings.

38. As it is used in lines 92–93, the phrase "searching for the location of a bad odor" most specifically refers to:

F. the use of magnetic fields to determine location.
G. using birds' scents to determine locations where they have traveled.
H. the raw sensory input used by birds.
J. the skill of olfactory navigation.

39. The main idea of the first paragraph is that:

A. the Arctic Tern has a particularly long migrational distance.
B. birds offer little useful information about navigation for humans.
C. the names given to birds do not accurately describe them.
D. birds are able to successfully navigate as they fly long distances.

40. The passage indicates that the primary theory behind bird navigation is that birds:

F. depend on their sense of sight to see the ground below.
G. rely on their sense of smell to navigate their environments.
H. are able to use multiple senses based on their unique circumstances.
J. use the magnetic fields in the ground to map their position.

STOP: END OF TEST 3

7.1 Answer Key

<table>
<tr><th>Question Number</th><th>Correct Answer</th><th>Question Type</th><th>Question Tier</th></tr>
<tr><td colspan="4">LITERARY NARRATIVE</td></tr>
<tr><td>1</td><td>D</td><td>Main Idea</td><td>2</td></tr>
<tr><td colspan="4">A. Although the passage is about Jane’s feelings about going back to school, it is not written in first-person.
B. The passage focuses on one character’s feelings about going back to school.
C. Jane’s mother and brother are briefly mentioned, but they are not the focus of the passage.
D. Throughout the passage, the main character’s summer is described, including “lazy afternoons in the backyard” (lines 21–22) and the trip to Barcelona (lines 28–29).</td></tr>
<tr><td>2</td><td>H</td><td>Specific Detail</td><td>1</td></tr>
<tr><td colspan="4">In lines 70–73, Jane feels “so stressed about the amount of work” that she “couldn’t even start to do it,” showing that she understood that she was being irrational. Jane knows her nervousness about school is silly, which makes her feel worse about her reaction.</td></tr>
<tr><td>3</td><td>D</td><td>Specific Detail</td><td>2</td></tr>
<tr><td colspan="4">Lines 7–12 state that a “step in the old routine” is for Jane to “sharpen her new box of pencils” in “the mechanical sharpener.”</td></tr>
<tr><td>4</td><td>G</td><td>Main Idea</td><td>2</td></tr>
<tr><td colspan="4">F. While Jane is nervous, she has taken time to prepare to return to school and isn’t frantic. It is not clear that she feels unhappy about returning to school.
G. The intro paragraph uses words like “nervous,” “jittery,” and “uneasiness” to show Jane’s feelings about returning to school.
H. Jane’s nerves show that she is not necessarily thrilled to return.
J. “Reckless” and “disapproving” are used to describe Jane’s mother’s feelings about her trip to Barcelona rather than Jane’s feelings about returning to school.</td></tr>
<tr><td>5</td><td>C</td><td>Purpose</td><td>1</td></tr>
<tr><td colspan="4">A. Paragraph 4 describes the neatness of Jane’s backpack and the supplies inside.
B. Paragraph 4 does not indicate Jane’s feelings about returning to school.
C. Paragraph 4 (lines 44–49) explains that “everything was arranged precisely in her backpack” and uses the pens as an example of that precision.
D. Paragraph 4 mentions polka dots to show the marks pens would leave if their caps weren’t on, which is not the purpose of this paragraph.</td></tr>
<tr><td>6</td><td>G</td><td>Specific Detail</td><td>2</td></tr>
<tr><td colspan="4">In lines 32–39, Jane’s mother calls her trip “reckless,” but Jane’s “stubbornness” means she knew she would be “getting on that plane anyways,” despite her mother’s disapproval.</td></tr>
</table>

<table>
<tr><th>Question Number</th><th>Correct Answer</th><th>Question Type</th><th>Question Tier</th></tr>
<tr><td>7</td><td>D</td><td>Purpose</td><td>1</td></tr>
<tr><td colspan="4">A. The paragraph mentions ”weeks and weeks of open schedules,” meaning there is no set routine.
B. The paragraph does not indicate that Jane worked at a pool.
C. The paragraph doesn’t argue that summer should be the start of the calendar year.
D. The paragraph describes Jane’s summer activities like relaxing in the backyard and swimming in the pool.</td></tr>
<tr><td>8</td><td>F</td><td>Specific Detail</td><td>2</td></tr>
<tr><td colspan="4">In lines 60–61, Jane thinks that “part of the struggle came from mourning the loss of summer.”</td></tr>
<tr><td>9</td><td>D</td><td>Main Idea</td><td>1</td></tr>
<tr><td colspan="4">A. The time Jane wakes up is a detail, not the main idea.
B. Jane’s classes are a detail, not the main idea.
C. Jane’s bus is a detail, not the main idea.
D. The conclusion of the paragraph states that “routine offered no reassurance,” explaining that Jane is still nervous even though she knows what to expect.</td></tr>
<tr><td>10</td><td>H</td><td>Specific Detail</td><td>2</td></tr>
<tr><td colspan="4">In line 42, Jack is described by his mother as having an “iron will.”</td></tr>
<tr><td colspan="4">SOCIAL SCIENCE</td></tr>
<tr><td>11</td><td>C</td><td>Main Idea</td><td>2</td></tr>
<tr><td colspan="4">A. This represents one theory among many, not the main idea.
B. The answer paraphrases one complication critics have noted but does not summarize the main idea of the passage.
C. The concluding paragraph summarizes the main idea: Democratic Peace Theory has potential, but also complications; further study is merited.
D. The passage suggests the goal is peace, not a balance between peace and war.</td></tr>
<tr><td>12</td><td>H</td><td>Purpose</td><td>1</td></tr>
<tr><td colspan="4">F. The question does not summarize any particular historic events.
G. The question does not offer an overview of possible strategies for promoting peace.
H. The question simply introduces the central concern Democratic Peace Theory attempts to address.
J. The question raises a concern, it doesn’t advance an argument.</td></tr>
<tr><td>13</td><td>A</td><td>Specific Detail</td><td>1</td></tr>
<tr><td colspan="4">Lines 69–71 state that an essential calculus has “either averted or necessitated war. . . ” “Averted” in this case must be the opposite of “necessitated,” which means “made necessary.” Thus, one synonym for “averted” could be “avoided.”</td></tr>
<tr><td>14</td><td>J</td><td>Specific Detail</td><td>2</td></tr>
<tr><td colspan="4">Lines 34–38 state: “A world of democracies might even do away with warfare altogether. This general premise is not a bad summary of the ideals...that have governed Western international relations since World War II.”</td></tr>
</table>

<table>
<tr><th>Question Number</th><th>Correct Answer</th><th>Question Type</th><th>Question Tier</th></tr>
<tr><td>15</td><td>C</td><td>Specific Detail</td><td>2</td></tr>
<tr><td colspan="4">Lines 48–50 state: “The claim, however, is not that democracies are generally peaceful, but rather that conflicts between democracies rarely escalate into true warfare.”</td></tr>
<tr><td>16</td><td>H</td><td>Specific Detail</td><td>2</td></tr>
<tr><td colspan="4">Lines 72–74 state: “The idea that a democracy, regardless of who is in power, would not first and foremost seek survival and security as naïve.”</td></tr>
<tr><td>17</td><td>C</td><td>Specific Detail</td><td>2</td></tr>
<tr><td colspan="4">Lines 24–26 state: “The theory has gained a strong foothold in universities, as well as amongst diplomats. . . ”</td></tr>
<tr><td>18</td><td>G</td><td>Specific Detail</td><td>3</td></tr>
<tr><td colspan="4">F. Lines 80–81 state “Perhaps peace depends more on economics...:”
G. The passage does not mention scholarship as a factor that correlates with or leads to peace.
H. Lines 83–84 state: “Or perhaps peace depends more on culture. . . ”
J. The passage as a whole discusses the possibility that democracy may lead to peace.</td></tr>
<tr><td>19</td><td>A</td><td>Purpose</td><td>1</td></tr>
<tr><td colspan="4">A. The first sentence begins with a contrast, signaling a shift. It then asserts that some critics disagree with Democratic Peace Theory. The paragraph explains the critique.
B. The paragraph does not provide any specific countries as examples.
C. The paragraph includes contrasting hypotheses as details, not the main idea.
D. The paragraph does not prove any points, even those it mentions.</td></tr>
<tr><td>20</td><td>H</td><td>Specific Detail</td><td>2</td></tr>
<tr><td colspan="4">Lines 46–48 state: “The 20th century is replete with conflict, even violence, resulting from disputes between democratic nations.”</td></tr>
<tr><td colspan="4">HUMANITIES</td></tr>
<tr><td>21</td><td>C</td><td>Specific Detail</td><td>3</td></tr>
<tr><td colspan="4">A. Line 39 mentions “a New York taxi horn.”
B. Line 9 mentions “chatter of passerby” as a sound in Central Park.
C. Lines 26–27 discuss “the structure of polka,” but not in the context of New York.
D. Line 10 mentions “bird calls” as a sound in Central Park.</td></tr>
<tr><td>22</td><td>G</td><td>Specific Detail</td><td>1</td></tr>
<tr><td colspan="4">Lines 19–20 state that the author hears “some hint of the composer’s nation, his travels...where he has lived” in a composition, indicating that the symphony reveals the composer’s history.</td></tr>
<tr><td>23</td><td>C</td><td>Specific Detail</td><td>2</td></tr>
<tr><td colspan="4">Lines 24–25 make the point that “music is deeply rooted...in culture.” The following sentences gives examples of compositions that show the composer’s culture.</td></tr>
<tr><td>24</td><td>J</td><td>Specific Detail</td><td>2</td></tr>
<tr><td colspan="4">In lines 69–71, the passage states that Monica Sayles describes her home as “the direct inspiration for... her compositions.”</td></tr>
</table>

Question Number	Correct Answer	Question Type	Question Tier
25	C	Purpose	1
A. The sentence implies that music can be equally popular regardless of the location where it was composed. **B.** The sentence does not mention specific examples of famous compositions. **C.** The passage states that works in those different cities "play to equal acclaim," indicating that they are popular among audiences who live outside of where they were composed. **D.** The sentence does not mention differences in the music based on location.			
26	J	Specific Detail	2
Line 48 states that "to transcend borders, a novel must be translated."			
27	B	Specific Detail	2
Lines 54–56 indicate that a musical composition "seems to pull at the same heartstrings, instill the same fear, inspire the same euphoria..."			
28	F	Main Idea	2
F. Passage A is written in the first person from a composer's point of view (line 37: "in my own compositions"). Passage B compares music to visual art and writing (Paragraph 1 mentions "a novel" and "visual art"). **G.** Passage A discusses how music is related to the context of the composer. Passage B talks about how music can be universally appreciated, regardless of context. **H.** While the author of Passage A composes in New York, they also mention compositions from around the world. Passage B uses the example of a composer in California but focuses mainly on the universality of music. **J.** Passage A focuses more on compositions than on audiences. Passage B mentions critics only to make a point about the universality of music.			
29	D	Specific Detail	2
In Passage A, lines 39–40 mention that "a clanging trash can or a New York taxi horn might find its way ...to the symphony hall." Nontraditional sounds are not discussed in Passage B.			
30	G	Specific Detail	2
In lines 43–44, Passage A states that "sounds that are specific" to a particular geographical context "become universal." In lines 98–100, Passage B states, "melody's ability to circumvent literal thought and tap directly into emotion lends music its seeming universality."			
NATURAL SCIENCE			
31	B	Purpose	2
A. Infrasound is a detail in the passage, not the main purpose. **B.** The conclusion states that "a bird can utilize a wealth of sensory input to chart and navigate its world." **C.** Birds carrying messages is a detail in the passage, not the main idea. **D.** The passage does not clearly identify which birds navigate the longest distances.			
32	F	Specific Detail	2
Lines 45–47 state, "scientists look not to their navigational success, but rather to controlled studies of their navigational failures."			

Question Number	Correct Answer	Question Type	Question Tier
33	B	Purpose	1
A. The "compass" is a theory rather than a physical compass. **B.** The second paragraph introduces the "map and compass" model for how birds navigate. The "map" is discussed in detail in later paragraphs. **C.** The paragraph does not describe a particular study. **D.** The "map and compass" model is not refuted in the passage.			
34	H	Specific Detail	3
F. Line 41 mentions "news of the early Greek Olympic games." **G.** Line 40 mentions "invasions of Genghis Khan." **H.** The passage does not indicate that pigeons carried maps. **J.** Lines 42–43 mention "codes from Allied forces invading Normandy during World War I."			
35	D	Specific Detail	2
Lines 29–32 state that "While the mechanisms behind the compass feature...are well-explained, the underlying mechanisms of the map feature remain widely debated."			
36	F	Specific Detail	1
Lines 58–61 discuss how low-frequency sound waves allow pigeons to construct, or create, maps of their surroundings. The pigeons create a mental picture, but they are not physically building or writing anything.			
37	B	Specific Detail	2
Lines 61–64 indicate that "when infrasound is disrupted...the homing pigeons' ability to navigate...is significantly diminished."			
38	J	Specific Detail	1
Lines 83–85 describe pigeons' ability to orient themselves "according to the position and density of odors, a skill known as olfactory navigation."			
39	D	Main Idea	1
A. The Arctic Tern is one detail, not the main idea of the paragraph. **B.** Birds are described in lines 1–2 as "the Earth's greatest navigators" in the paragraph. **C.** The names of birds are not the main idea of the paragraph. **D.** The conclusion sentence in lines 11–12 states that "when it comes to navigation," birds are "the true experts..."			
40	H	Specific Detail	2
In the conclusion paragraph, line 87–88 state that "different birds may use different senses to navigate in different circumstances."			

Raw Score: ___ / 40

Converted Score: ___ / 36

7.2 Scoring Rubric

Score Conversion[1]

Scaled Score	Raw Score	Raw Score	Scaled Score
1	0	19	**19**
2	–	20–21	**20**
3	1	22	**21**
4	2	23–24	**22**
5	–	25	**23**
6	3	26	**24**
7	–	27	**25**
8	4	28	**26**
9	5	29	**27**
10	6	30	**28**
11	7	31	**29**
12	8–9	32	**30**
13	10–11	33	**31**
14	12	34–35	**32**
15	13–14	36	**33**
16	15	37	**34**
17	16	38	**35**
18	17–18	39–40	**36**

[1]Score Conversions are general estimates based on the average correlations between raw scores and scaled scores as seen on recent ACT exams. They are meant to be used as such: general estimates.

Chapter 8

Extended Time Accommodations

If you have an accommodation that grants extended time, your approach to the ACT Reading section might differ somewhat (but not entirely!) from what is outlined in this book. Generally, you will be using the same strategies, but there are a few key differences:

Section Timing

- National Extended Time: Time-and-a-Half on One Day. You will have 1.5 x the standard time, giving you **55 minutes** to complete the Reading section of the ACT.
- Multiple Day Testing: Some accommodations allow you to test across multiple days, meaning that you will work through each section of the test (English, Math, Reading, and Science), or two sections of the test, in different sittings. In terms of time limits, you may be granted...
  - Time-and-a-Half: 55 minutes for Reading
  - Double Time: 70 minutes = 1 hour and 10 minutes for Reading
  - Triple Time: 105 minutes = 1 hour and 45 minutes for Reading

Splitting Your Time

You want to be strategic about how to use your additional time. After all, the minutes are yours, and you can use them however you want. The key is to experiment with a few different options to find which one maximizes your score. Broadly speaking, you have two basic options to try:

- Use (most of) your additional time on the Questions

  You may decide to spend your additional time dealing with the questions, rather than allotting the extra time to reading the passages. In this case, you still "read" (skim, outline etc) the passages quickly, then spend most of your time finding answers to the questions. The strategies from "The Read" (Chapter 4) will help you read more quickly and efficiently.

- Use (most of) your additional time on the Passages

  Alternatively, you may find it's more helpful to spend your additional time reading entire passages for all (or some) of the passage types. If additional reading time helps to improve your overall comprehension, it might be worth it. If your overall comprehension of a passage does improve with additional reading time, you will be able to answer questions more quickly and confidently. Quick note: Reading the entire passage can be especially useful for the Literary Narrative and/or Humanities passages.

Using This Book

Keep your timing accommodations in mind when working through this book. While Chapter Tests and Practice Tests may have given time limits, time yourself according to how you've planned your extended time.

Timing by The Read – Chapter 4 (p. 73)

Standard Time	Time-and-a-Half	Double Time	Triple Time
Read-it-All Method: 3 minutes or less	4.5 minutes	6 minutes	9 minutes
Outline Method: 2 minutes or less	3 minutes	4 minutes	6 minutes
2/3 Method: 3 minutes or less	4.5 minutes	6 minutes	9 minutes

Timing Per Passage – Chapter 4 (p. 73)

Standard Time	Time-and-a-Half	Double Time	Triple Time
9, 9, 9, 8 minutes	14, 14, 14, 13	18, 18, 18, 16	27, 27, 27, 24
11, 8, 8, 8 minutes	16, 13, 13, 13	22, 16, 16, 16	33, 24, 24, 24
10, 10, 10, 5 minutes	15, 15, 15, 10	20, 20, 20, 10	30, 30, 30, 15
11, 11, 11, 2 minutes	16, 16, 16, 7	22, 22, 22, 4	33, 33, 33, 6

Chapter 9

Computer-Based Testing

The ACT offers Computer-Based Testing, or CBT, to those who take the test internationally. While most of the tactics you've learned throughout this book still apply, small differences exist.

The tools provided directly on the interface of the CBT are as follows:

- **Test Timer** on the upper right-hand corner tells you how much time is left in each subject.
- **Magnifier** menu allows you to enlarge text.
- **Highlighter** acts as, of course, a highlighter.
- **Line Reader** separates a single line of text so you can more easily focus on it.
- **Answer Eliminator** lets you cross out answers that you think are incorrect.
- **Answer Masking** hides answer choices until you click on them.

Some of these tools are more helpful than others. Here are some guidelines to best use each one:

- At the beginning of the section, turn on the **Answer Eliminator** under the "Tools" dropdown. Then, you can x-out any answer choices you would like to eliminate, working as part of the **process of elimination** tactic (page 84).
- Also immediately turn on the **Answer Masking** tool. Doing so will give you a physical reminder to **anticipate** answers whenever possible (page 46).
- Annotating the text isn't an option with CBT, and it is important to note that whatever you highlight does **not** carry over from question to question. In other words, if you highlight text during Question 1, you won't see what you've highlighted when you move on to Question 2. Instead, focus on creating a **textual map** on the sheet of paper given to you for notes. Look back to page 23 for instructions on just how to do that.
- You may find it too confusing to scroll back and forth between questions to use the Tier system (page 79). If so, it is fine to **complete questions in order**—the trick from the previous bullet will save you some extra time.

Most importantly, make sure to visit the official ACT website to try out these tools before your test date. That way, you can make sure to already have a handle on which tools you prefer to use, how to use those tools, and which tools you can do without.

Chapter 10

Answer Sheets

On the following pages, you'll find scantron-style answer sheets. Tear them out to record your answers if you'd like to replicate the full test-taking experience on the Chapter 4 Test or Practice Tests 1–3.

Test ____

1 (A) (B) (C) (D)	11 (A) (B) (C) (D)	21 (A) (B) (C) (D)	31 (A) (B) (C) (D)
2 (F) (G) (H) (J)	12 (F) (G) (H) (J)	22 (F) (G) (H) (J)	32 (F) (G) (H) (J)
3 (A) (B) (C) (D)	13 (A) (B) (C) (D)	23 (A) (B) (C) (D)	33 (A) (B) (C) (D)
4 (F) (G) (H) (J)	14 (F) (G) (H) (J)	24 (F) (G) (H) (J)	34 (F) (G) (H) (J)
5 (A) (B) (C) (D)	15 (A) (B) (C) (D)	25 (A) (B) (C) (D)	35 (A) (B) (C) (D)
6 (F) (G) (H) (J)	16 (F) (G) (H) (J)	26 (F) (G) (H) (J)	36 (F) (G) (H) (J)
7 (A) (B) (C) (D)	17 (A) (B) (C) (D)	27 (A) (B) (C) (D)	37 (A) (B) (C) (D)
8 (F) (G) (H) (J)	18 (F) (G) (H) (J)	28 (F) (G) (H) (J)	38 (F) (G) (H) (J)
9 (A) (B) (C) (D)	19 (A) (B) (C) (D)	29 (A) (B) (C) (D)	39 (A) (B) (C) (D)
10 (F) (G) (H) (J)	20 (F) (G) (H) (J)	30 (F) (G) (H) (J)	40 (F) (G) (H) (J)

Test ____

1 (A) (B) (C) (D)	11 (A) (B) (C) (D)	21 (A) (B) (C) (D)	31 (A) (B) (C) (D)
2 (F) (G) (H) (J)	12 (F) (G) (H) (J)	22 (F) (G) (H) (J)	32 (F) (G) (H) (J)
3 (A) (B) (C) (D)	13 (A) (B) (C) (D)	23 (A) (B) (C) (D)	33 (A) (B) (C) (D)
4 (F) (G) (H) (J)	14 (F) (G) (H) (J)	24 (F) (G) (H) (J)	34 (F) (G) (H) (J)
5 (A) (B) (C) (D)	15 (A) (B) (C) (D)	25 (A) (B) (C) (D)	35 (A) (B) (C) (D)
6 (F) (G) (H) (J)	16 (F) (G) (H) (J)	26 (F) (G) (H) (J)	36 (F) (G) (H) (J)
7 (A) (B) (C) (D)	17 (A) (B) (C) (D)	27 (A) (B) (C) (D)	37 (A) (B) (C) (D)
8 (F) (G) (H) (J)	18 (F) (G) (H) (J)	28 (F) (G) (H) (J)	38 (F) (G) (H) (J)
9 (A) (B) (C) (D)	19 (A) (B) (C) (D)	29 (A) (B) (C) (D)	39 (A) (B) (C) (D)
10 (F) (G) (H) (J)	20 (F) (G) (H) (J)	30 (F) (G) (H) (J)	40 (F) (G) (H) (J)

Test ____

1 (A) (B) (C) (D)	11 (A) (B) (C) (D)	21 (A) (B) (C) (D)	31 (A) (B) (C) (D)
2 (F) (G) (H) (J)	12 (F) (G) (H) (J)	22 (F) (G) (H) (J)	32 (F) (G) (H) (J)
3 (A) (B) (C) (D)	13 (A) (B) (C) (D)	23 (A) (B) (C) (D)	33 (A) (B) (C) (D)
4 (F) (G) (H) (J)	14 (F) (G) (H) (J)	24 (F) (G) (H) (J)	34 (F) (G) (H) (J)
5 (A) (B) (C) (D)	15 (A) (B) (C) (D)	25 (A) (B) (C) (D)	35 (A) (B) (C) (D)
6 (F) (G) (H) (J)	16 (F) (G) (H) (J)	26 (F) (G) (H) (J)	36 (F) (G) (H) (J)
7 (A) (B) (C) (D)	17 (A) (B) (C) (D)	27 (A) (B) (C) (D)	37 (A) (B) (C) (D)
8 (F) (G) (H) (J)	18 (F) (G) (H) (J)	28 (F) (G) (H) (J)	38 (F) (G) (H) (J)
9 (A) (B) (C) (D)	19 (A) (B) (C) (D)	29 (A) (B) (C) (D)	39 (A) (B) (C) (D)
10 (F) (G) (H) (J)	20 (F) (G) (H) (J)	30 (F) (G) (H) (J)	40 (F) (G) (H) (J)

Test ____

1 (A) (B) (C) (D)	11 (A) (B) (C) (D)	21 (A) (B) (C) (D)	31 (A) (B) (C) (D)
2 (F) (G) (H) (J)	12 (F) (G) (H) (J)	22 (F) (G) (H) (J)	32 (F) (G) (H) (J)
3 (A) (B) (C) (D)	13 (A) (B) (C) (D)	23 (A) (B) (C) (D)	33 (A) (B) (C) (D)
4 (F) (G) (H) (J)	14 (F) (G) (H) (J)	24 (F) (G) (H) (J)	34 (F) (G) (H) (J)
5 (A) (B) (C) (D)	15 (A) (B) (C) (D)	25 (A) (B) (C) (D)	35 (A) (B) (C) (D)
6 (F) (G) (H) (J)	16 (F) (G) (H) (J)	26 (F) (G) (H) (J)	36 (F) (G) (H) (J)
7 (A) (B) (C) (D)	17 (A) (B) (C) (D)	27 (A) (B) (C) (D)	37 (A) (B) (C) (D)
8 (F) (G) (H) (J)	18 (F) (G) (H) (J)	28 (F) (G) (H) (J)	38 (F) (G) (H) (J)
9 (A) (B) (C) (D)	19 (A) (B) (C) (D)	29 (A) (B) (C) (D)	39 (A) (B) (C) (D)
10 (F) (G) (H) (J)	20 (F) (G) (H) (J)	30 (F) (G) (H) (J)	40 (F) (G) (H) (J)

Test ____

1 (A) (B) (C) (D)	11 (A) (B) (C) (D)	21 (A) (B) (C) (D)	31 (A) (B) (C) (D)
2 (F) (G) (H) (J)	12 (F) (G) (H) (J)	22 (F) (G) (H) (J)	32 (F) (G) (H) (J)
3 (A) (B) (C) (D)	13 (A) (B) (C) (D)	23 (A) (B) (C) (D)	33 (A) (B) (C) (D)
4 (F) (G) (H) (J)	14 (F) (G) (H) (J)	24 (F) (G) (H) (J)	34 (F) (G) (H) (J)
5 (A) (B) (C) (D)	15 (A) (B) (C) (D)	25 (A) (B) (C) (D)	35 (A) (B) (C) (D)
6 (F) (G) (H) (J)	16 (F) (G) (H) (J)	26 (F) (G) (H) (J)	36 (F) (G) (H) (J)
7 (A) (B) (C) (D)	17 (A) (B) (C) (D)	27 (A) (B) (C) (D)	37 (A) (B) (C) (D)
8 (F) (G) (H) (J)	18 (F) (G) (H) (J)	28 (F) (G) (H) (J)	38 (F) (G) (H) (J)
9 (A) (B) (C) (D)	19 (A) (B) (C) (D)	29 (A) (B) (C) (D)	39 (A) (B) (C) (D)
10 (F) (G) (H) (J)	20 (F) (G) (H) (J)	30 (F) (G) (H) (J)	40 (F) (G) (H) (J)

Test ____

1 (A) (B) (C) (D)	11 (A) (B) (C) (D)	21 (A) (B) (C) (D)	31 (A) (B) (C) (D)
2 (F) (G) (H) (J)	12 (F) (G) (H) (J)	22 (F) (G) (H) (J)	32 (F) (G) (H) (J)
3 (A) (B) (C) (D)	13 (A) (B) (C) (D)	23 (A) (B) (C) (D)	33 (A) (B) (C) (D)
4 (F) (G) (H) (J)	14 (F) (G) (H) (J)	24 (F) (G) (H) (J)	34 (F) (G) (H) (J)
5 (A) (B) (C) (D)	15 (A) (B) (C) (D)	25 (A) (B) (C) (D)	35 (A) (B) (C) (D)
6 (F) (G) (H) (J)	16 (F) (G) (H) (J)	26 (F) (G) (H) (J)	36 (F) (G) (H) (J)
7 (A) (B) (C) (D)	17 (A) (B) (C) (D)	27 (A) (B) (C) (D)	37 (A) (B) (C) (D)
8 (F) (G) (H) (J)	18 (F) (G) (H) (J)	28 (F) (G) (H) (J)	38 (F) (G) (H) (J)
9 (A) (B) (C) (D)	19 (A) (B) (C) (D)	29 (A) (B) (C) (D)	39 (A) (B) (C) (D)
10 (F) (G) (H) (J)	20 (F) (G) (H) (J)	30 (F) (G) (H) (J)	40 (F) (G) (H) (J)

Test ____

1 A B C D	11 A B C D	21 A B C D	31 A B C D
2 F G H J	12 F G H J	22 F G H J	32 F G H J
3 A B C D	13 A B C D	23 A B C D	33 A B C D
4 F G H J	14 F G H J	24 F G H J	34 F G H J
5 A B C D	15 A B C D	25 A B C D	35 A B C D
6 F G H J	16 F G H J	26 F G H J	36 F G H J
7 A B C D	17 A B C D	27 A B C D	37 A B C D
8 F G H J	18 F G H J	28 F G H J	38 F G H J
9 A B C D	19 A B C D	29 A B C D	39 A B C D
10 F G H J	20 F G H J	30 F G H J	40 F G H J

Test ____

1 A B C D	11 A B C D	21 A B C D	31 A B C D
2 F G H J	12 F G H J	22 F G H J	32 F G H J
3 A B C D	13 A B C D	23 A B C D	33 A B C D
4 F G H J	14 F G H J	24 F G H J	34 F G H J
5 A B C D	15 A B C D	25 A B C D	35 A B C D
6 F G H J	16 F G H J	26 F G H J	36 F G H J
7 A B C D	17 A B C D	27 A B C D	37 A B C D
8 F G H J	18 F G H J	28 F G H J	38 F G H J
9 A B C D	19 A B C D	29 A B C D	39 A B C D
10 F G H J	20 F G H J	30 F G H J	40 F G H J

Test ____

1 A B C D	11 A B C D	21 A B C D	31 A B C D
2 F G H J	12 F G H J	22 F G H J	32 F G H J
3 A B C D	13 A B C D	23 A B C D	33 A B C D
4 F G H J	14 F G H J	24 F G H J	34 F G H J
5 A B C D	15 A B C D	25 A B C D	35 A B C D
6 F G H J	16 F G H J	26 F G H J	36 F G H J
7 A B C D	17 A B C D	27 A B C D	37 A B C D
8 F G H J	18 F G H J	28 F G H J	38 F G H J
9 A B C D	19 A B C D	29 A B C D	39 A B C D
10 F G H J	20 F G H J	30 F G H J	40 F G H J

Test ______________________________

1 A B C D
2 F G H J
3 A B C D
4 F G H J
5 A B C D
6 F G H J
7 A B C D
8 F G H J
9 A B C D
10 F G H J
11 A B C D
12 F G H J
13 A B C D
14 F G H J
15 A B C D
16 F G H J
17 A B C D
18 F G H J
19 A B C D
20 F G H J
21 A B C D
22 F G H J
23 A B C D
24 F G H J
25 A B C D
26 F G H J
27 A B C D
28 F G H J
29 A B C D
30 F G H J
31 A B C D
32 F G H J
33 A B C D
34 F G H J
35 A B C D
36 F G H J
37 A B C D
38 F G H J
39 A B C D
40 F G H J

Test ______________________________

1 A B C D
2 F G H J
3 A B C D
4 F G H J
5 A B C D
6 F G H J
7 A B C D
8 F G H J
9 A B C D
10 F G H J
11 A B C D
12 F G H J
13 A B C D
14 F G H J
15 A B C D
16 F G H J
17 A B C D
18 F G H J
19 A B C D
20 F G H J
21 A B C D
22 F G H J
23 A B C D
24 F G H J
25 A B C D
26 F G H J
27 A B C D
28 F G H J
29 A B C D
30 F G H J
31 A B C D
32 F G H J
33 A B C D
34 F G H J
35 A B C D
36 F G H J
37 A B C D
38 F G H J
39 A B C D
40 F G H J

Test ______________________________

1 A B C D
2 F G H J
3 A B C D
4 F G H J
5 A B C D
6 F G H J
7 A B C D
8 F G H J
9 A B C D
10 F G H J
11 A B C D
12 F G H J
13 A B C D
14 F G H J
15 A B C D
16 F G H J
17 A B C D
18 F G H J
19 A B C D
20 F G H J
21 A B C D
22 F G H J
23 A B C D
24 F G H J
25 A B C D
26 F G H J
27 A B C D
28 F G H J
29 A B C D
30 F G H J
31 A B C D
32 F G H J
33 A B C D
34 F G H J
35 A B C D
36 F G H J
37 A B C D
38 F G H J
39 A B C D
40 F G H J

Private Prep is an education services company that offers individually customized lessons in all K-12 academic subjects, standardized test prep, and college admissions consulting. We believe personal attention is fundamental to academic achievement and lies at the forefront of every student-tutor relationship. Designing curriculum for each student's unique learning style, we focus not only on improving grades and increasing test scores but also on building confidence and developing valuable skills—like work ethic, growth mindset, and anxiety management—that will last a lifetime.

One of the most significant points of differentiation between us and other educational services companies is our team approach. Our directors work in tandem with tutors and support staff to provide comprehensive, collaborative support to families.

We also focus on giving back to the communities in which we work. Through the Private Prep Scholarship Program, we place high-achieving students from low-income or underserved backgrounds with individual tutors, who work with them to navigate the test prep and college application process and ultimately gain admission to best-fit colleges.

At Private Prep, we deliver a superior academic experience—in the U.S., abroad, and online—that is supported by diverse and excellent resources in recruitment, curriculum design, professional training, and custom software development.

Made in USA - Kendallville, IN
39921_9780996832274
07.07.2022 1407